I'm a Big Boy Now

I'm a Big Boy Now

Eamon O'Leary

Bridge House

British Library Cataloguing in Publication Data
A Record of this Publication is available from the British
Library

ISBN 978-1-914199-64-6

This edition published 2024 by Bridge House Publishing
Manchester, England

Contents

Introduction

Imagine a world before the internet. Before smartphones. Before a hundred channels on a flat-screen TV, and a round-the-clock news cycle pumping out endless, depressing stories.

Imagine a world that quiet. That peaceful. That completely different from the here and now.

Let me, in *I'm A Big Boy Now*, take you into that world. The world of an Irish childhood in the late 50s and 1960s. An age when we gathered our mates by walking round to their places. When we rode our bikes together for hours. When we found adventure, or mischief, or both, any chance we could – and if it wasn't there, we invented it.

A time of cowboys, home-made go-karts, and all the lessons that go into becoming a *Big Boy*. Even towards the end, the dreaded Lesson About Girls.

You'll meet my family – Ma, Da, and the Brother as I chronicle, not just the lessons and adventures that turned me into a *Big Boy*, but also the air of the time and place that was 1960s Ireland. As we travel from Dublin to Kerry, from Roscommon to Cork, all the laughs are amplified, all the privations normalized, through the eyes of someone who was just trying to have as much fun as possible.

Setting the house on fire was just a mistake!

When the 21st century feels too hectic, too busy, too loud, grab a glass of something warming and let me take you back to a quieter world, where family, friends, and fun were all there was. A world of walkable boundaries and unlimited imagination.

Like everyone else, I did the Growing Up bit only once. Reading *I'm A Big Boy Now*, I hope you'll do it again and again, for the love, the laughs, and the life of a boy growing up with an endless thirst for adventure.

Part 1

The Dubs

Technicolour Blues

It was hard to put an age on Jake. Sitting tall in the saddle, unshaved, and sweaty, he swept a layer of grime and dust from his well-travelled cotton shirt. Then he ran his enormous, calloused hands through his brown hair.

Those hands could do damage.

With care, he replaced the wide-brimmed Stetson low over his wrinkled forehead. His feisty white mare stood impatiently, pawing the dirt with her left front hoof.

Jake had gone West years earlier, intending to farm the land.

He had failed. Drought, disease, and loneliness had taken their toll. Nowadays, he led wagon trains of hopefuls; mostly Dutch, Irish, and Scottish emigrants, with a sprinkling of poor Americans who'd nothing but the clothes on their backs. Banded together for protection, they hoped to build new lives for themselves and their families on the hostile, lawless frontier.

Jake had made the trip from Elm Grove, Missouri many times, but today, on the South Pass, short of the Snake River, something didn't seem right. Tumbleweed and wild grasses danced in the furnace heat. The air the same as always, clean, and earthy. He watched and waited till, through the shimmering warmth, a lone rider approached. It was Eagle Heart, his trusted Indian scout.

"All is quiet," he said, jumping from his unsaddled, polka-dotted Appaloosa.

Maybe too quiet, thought Jake. Again, they scoured the high, sand-coloured rocks on both sides of the gorge. Not a sound except the warm breeze that whistled, then sighed as it blew through the Pass.

They rode to where the wagon train waited. Women held their children close. Husbands busied themselves with chores, trying to conceal their fear.

"All's clear," said Jake. "Get them wagons rolling and don't stop for nothin' till you reach the other end of the canyon."

The lead wagon was halfway through when the attack came.

Whoosh. A salvo of steel-tipped arrows streaked through the air, hitting their targets with deadly force. With a crimson stream flowing from his chest, the man at the reins of the leading wagon fell forward into the dust, and his neck broke on impact. The wagon veered like the horses were drunk with freedom, then overturned. And then the screaming started. Screaming crazed Apache thundered into the Pass. Geronimo had kept his promise: "No more white men will cross the lands where our spirits rest." It looked as if hundreds, maybe thousands, of his braves had answered the call.

Panic was instant.

"Get the wagons in a circle. Get 'em in a circle!" roared Jake.

They had no chance. Flaming arrows scorched through the hot, dry air. Within seconds, the wagons were ablaze. Jake took a hit to the shoulder but hung on. Eagle Heart wasn't so lucky. He fell to the swipe of a tomahawk and was trampled by ponies as hysterical as their riders. Thunderous noise echoed off the walls of the valley, making it sound like something had trapped them inside a death-drum. Louder than the screeching of the Apache were the pathetic screams of the women and children as they tried to find cover that didn't exist.

One piercing voice, however, drowned out everything.

That was Me.

It was our first time in the Adelphi Cinema Dublin. Da held me in his arms.

"It's only a film, Son, it's only pretending."

11

I continued to wail, Da's words meaningless against the pictures on the screen. Before me were flames and blood. Men, women, and children screaming.

"Hey, mister, will you take the poor child outta here? Can't you see he's scared?" came from the row behind us.

My eyes blinked when we hit the afternoon sun on O'Connell Street, where normal Saturday life was in progress. Buses belched fumes, horns honked and shoppers, mostly women, lugged bags laden with groceries.

"There now," Da said, holding my hand. "The pictures are only makey-uppy."

Makey-uppy. O'Connell Street was still there. Still real. There were no Apache riding down from Woolworths to murder us. My frantic blinking slowed. It was alright. Everything was alright.

"This is all new technology, Son. Technicolour makes everything look more realistic, but it's only make-believe."

I didn't know what he was talking about. All I knew was I could practically feel those flames, could still almost feel the blood leaking out of the dead man's chest. But Da said it was OK, so problem solved. We returned and took our seats next to Ma and the big Brother.

But it wasn't long before Geronimo and his mates gave it one more lash. I launched into the vocals once again. The mood around us had changed. Gone was the sympathy for the "poor child".

"Hey, mister, will you take that feckin' thick eejit of a young fella outta here?"

This time, we all left and got the bus. Da didn't have to pay for himself because he worked for the bus and train people. He should have been smiling because he knew the conductor, who winked and didn't charge for us, but Da's eyes were popping out of his head. He loved westerns and had skipped a few visits to the Submarine bar to take us. It was one of the first films to have this new Technicolour thing.

After a few minutes' silence, I asked, "Hey Da, will Jake and the little boys and girls be OK?"

I'll never forget the way he looked at me. His forehead told of worries present and worries for the future. He lit a cigarette but said nothing. The Brother laughed; I began whinging. Da lashed out and gave the Brother a backhander, and then *he* started bawling. Then, never one to be left out of a drama, Ma joined in, sniffling and wiping away tears. "Why can't we be like every other family?"

Everyone cried except for Da. He sighed.

Thus ended another normal family outing.

Later, when the wailing had died down a bit, I washed my face and teeth and put on my pyjamas, and Da read me a story from *The Beano*. Then he gave me a big hug and kissed me on the forehead. He'd never done that before.

March 1957. I was four and two-thirds on that momentous day.

Ten years passed before Da took me to the pictures again.

Bells a-Ringing.

The wind shook the windows and because it was lashing and because I was a big boy of four and three-quarters, Ma said she'd leave me at home when she went to the shops.

"I'll be back in ten minutes. I'm only going to the butchers to get a few chops. Promise me you'll be a good boy, and I'll bring you home a Trigger bar."

"Yes, Ma."

Wow! All alone in the house for the very first time, but ten minutes is a long time, and with hail pelting like bullets against the windows, I felt cold, so I crawled under my bed.

That's where I kept my treasure in a shoebox Da gave me. An enormous spider and two wasps wrapped in tissue paper, and a lump of bubble gum in a matchbox, and all my old *Beanos* were there as well. I thought a tiny fire would make it more comfy and darted to the kitchen where, after rummaging around, I found a box of matches hidden behind jars of Ma's blackberry jam. Ma and Da always said, "Never touch those."

But I was big now.

Back under the bed I went, emptied my valuables from the shoebox and half-filled it with scraps of paper from an ancient comic that had gone brown and smelly. Only little flames, but I soon warmed up, all nice and cosy until I heard someone kicking our door and shouting in the letterbox.

"Are you coming out? The rain's stopped and we can go up the field and play cowboys and Indi—"

My best friend, Kevin Coghlan. I reached on my tippy-toes, opened the door, grabbed my coat, dipped my fingers in the holy water, and rode off. Ma told me to bless myself every time I went out – "If you do," she said, "Jesus will look after you for the whole day."

Kevin, a year and a quarter older than me, hadn't started

school yet. He was nearly six. Maybe his ma kept him at home because he always had snail-shaped bubbles coming out his nose. Green they were. And he wiped them on his sleeves. That's why they were always shiny.

Ma once said, "I think he's a bit slow," but I told her Kev could run as fast as me. She threw her eyes to heaven and went back to washing shirts and underpants in the sink.

We gave our backsides a wallop and took off up the road to the woods. Me as The Lone Ranger, riding Silver, and Kevin at my side was Tonto on a pony. Sometimes Kevin wanted to be The Lone Ranger, but I told him I'd only be his best friend if *I* was.

Most people dumped their grass and sometimes other rubbish in the woods, and Ma didn't like us playing up there.

"It's too dangerous. You'd never know what kind of quare hawk might be wandering around." But Da said, "They'll be fine. It's sad, but in a few weeks, the bulldozers will be in, destroying in a few hours what's been growing for years. Let them enjoy the trees and the bit of grass while they can, because by next summer, it'll be houses and concrete they'll be playing on."

The day before, Me and Kev had made a camp in among the small trees with an old mattress we'd found but we couldn't play in it because it was soaking after all the rain, so Kev went climbing the biggest tree. Up he went like a squirrel. Someone told us it was an oak and probably hundreds of years old. It nearly reached the clouds.

"Tarzan, Tarzan, swinging on a rope, can't wash his ass, 'cos he has no soap."

Kev always sang that when he reached the top of a tree. I could climb as good as him, but stayed on the ground, keeping watch in case Geronimo or other Indians attacked.

"What's that noise?" I said, looking up.

15

"Me look," said Tonto. "It fire engines, two of them, coming down our road."

Seconds later, we were galloping towards the clanging bells. In the distance, we saw puffs of smoke, and I could see loads of the neighbours outside our bungalow, shouting and running around the place. A few were holding on to Ma. I couldn't make out all the screaming, but it sounded like; "My baby, my baby, my baby's in there."

"What's wrong, Ma?" I asked, panting after racing back.

I think Jesus must have been on a day off, and I didn't duck in time and my ears really hurt, and it took days before the swelling went down, and ages before I could hear again.

And then Ma announced, "It's time for school for you, my boy."

Previously published by Pure Slush Books.

Mango

Almost everyone on our road had a dog. Bullet was Kevin's dog, a massive one, bigger than Kevin and me put together. When he wasn't barking, he slobbered, panted, and farted. We called him Bullet because that's the name of Roy Rogers' dog. Supposed to be an Alsatian and a guard dog, he'd long thin legs like a greyhound and I heard Kevin's da cursing him once. He told my da, "That dog's a pure eejit. All he does is bark and wag his fecking tail. That tail is flying around non-stop. It's a wonder he doesn't take off. I'm telling ye, the fecker I bought him off is a right chancer. Thoroughbred, my arse. I think Bullet's mother played the field, if ye get my drift."

Da laughed and lit a fag, but I didn't understand what they were talking about.

But Bullet could run faster than anyone, and when Kevin put a collar on him, he'd shoot off, dragging Kevin, who skeeted along behind. He used his runners as brakes and his toes peeped out the top and his ma used to shout at him, "Are you thick or what?"

Da didn't like the man who moved into the house at the end of our road, just before the corner to the main road.

"Have you ever spoken to him?" Ma asked.

"No, but that doesn't matter. Anyone who calls their dog Hitler must be weird."

"I'm not sure who the weird one is." Ma said as she pulled a heap of Da's shirts from the kitchen sink.

"What's that you said?"

"Nothing."

"I'm telling you, he's weird. A bad-tempered, short-bodied, stumpy-legged bundle of sneaky misery. They're well matched, him and that flea-ridden mutt. Did you ever see the way he slinks along by the wall, his miserable face

17

almost touching the ground, his tail curled between his back legs?"

Ma knew better than to take on Da when he got a notion fixed in his head.

"Yes, Dear," she replied, hauling the shirts out to the clothesline.

We didn't have a dog. Instead, we had a cat who *thought* he was a dog. Nobody could tell how we came to own him. He had claws as long as spears and ears that looked like something had chewed them and spat them back out. With a nose all mashed in, he looked a right gurrier and Bullet kept out of his way. Da said, "He's a right hard chaw. When he purrs, it's worse than a dirty diesel engine." Rusty, yellow and brownish he was. Even uglier than Hitler.

"We'll have to give him a name," Da said. "Let's call him Mango for a laugh."

"What's a mango, Da?"

"Not sure. I think it's some kind of a fruit. They look lousy, but I read somewhere they are sweet and juicy."

"You can't call him that," Ma said. "That's a stupid name for a cat."

"It's better than Manky," Da said, and Ma could see the justice in that, so Mango he stayed.

The Sack Man

The bulldozers came in the Summer. Our trees and saplings didn't stand a chance. One by one, they fell like soldiers in battle, camps and hideaways gone in a day. All that remained was a brown slick the colour of gick.

"Where will the bird's nest?" Ma asked.

"They'll find somewhere," Da said. "Them builders don't give a shite. This place will never see green again. Houses eating up the land is the order of the day. Progress, my arse."

"Don't curse in front of the children."

Hammering, banging, more cursing, and shouting followed when the building started.

"Stay outta there, I'm warning the pair of you, it's dangerous," Ma ordered me and the Brother, but we sneaked up there anyway for a nose around. Planks longer than the trees they had chopped were lifted off lorries and load after load of grey concrete blocks got stacked where each bungalow would be built.

They may have knocked our woods, but they created the perfect playground for me, the Brother and the rest of our gang. The Brother was the leader because he was almost eight. I was five and a bit.

Half-built houses became our forts for cowboy games, and the trenches, our tunnels for battles. I could stand in the massive pipes and when we shouted, echoes bounced all around, and we played hide and seek as well. We created rifles from bits of timber left lying around, and even Da gathered piles of small chunks for firewood, although he waited till nighttime in case any of the neighbours were peeping out from behind the curtains.

The Brother got brave one evening after we'd had our tea, and after finding a ladder, climbed the scaffolding. I followed. The wind blew and rattled everything, and my legs shook, and I wanted to go back down, but the Brother said it was the perfect place to set an ambush.

I said "yeah," because when we played commandos, ambushes were allowed.

He crawled in between the rafters like a snake but stopped when he saw Da striding up the road.

"He'll kill us."

Then the Brother disappeared.

He'd jumped straight into the mud. I froze. Not enough time to get to the ladder, I thought, and headed to the edge. Da started running... "No, No, No, Son. Stay there. It's alright, just stay where you are," he shouted, waving his arms like a loony, "It's all right son, don't ju..."

I closed my eyes and took off, landing in the muck a few inches from a pile of concrete blocks.

Da said nothing. Instead, his face turned the colour of flour, and his hands shook. He lit a fag and drew a long drag before picking me up and carrying me home.

"Jeez, how many times have I told you to keep outta there?" Ma said. I thought we'd get a few wallops of the wooden spoon, but Da saved us.

"They're both OK," he said. "Will you make a cuppa tea and put a decent drop of Jameson into it?"

Soon after that, the builder got a night watchman, and although it was summer, he lit a fire every evening in a massive barrel with bullet-sized holes in it. After checking us guttersnipes weren't wandering around, he'd plonk himself down on a seat made from a few blocks and a plank and smoke his pipe. The Brother said his name was Christy. Well, Christy had to use a walking stick because he had a fierce limp. We gawked in at him most evenings until he said, "You can sit by the fire if you want."

In our khaki short trousers, we sat, legs crossed, arms

folded as Christy told us stories. Mango stretched out in front like a crocodile.

"Let me tell you, war isn't a game, and it's no fun," he said, before taking a long pull on his pipe and hoicking a noisy spit in the brazier's direction. He sucked the pipe a lot to give his tongue a rest, otherwise it waved in all directions.

He told us about fighting a guy called Rommel in the desert in Africa and getting shot and blown up.

The Brother took off.

"Did you have a machine gun, mister, and did you kill many of the enemy, and did you ever jump from a plane or fly a bomber and were you ever in a submarine?"

I think Christy was sorry he'd issued the invitation.

"Let me tell you, son, I don't want to talk about things I've seen or done. War is war, we'll leave it at that."

"It's probably all waffle," Da said when we told him about Christy's stories. "He doesn't look much like a soldier."

Not known for being shy, the Brother gave Christy both barrels the next evening.

"My Da says you're only making up all this war stuff."

Christy said nothing but took off his boot and rolled up his trousers. I nearly fell over. All he had was a shiny chunk of steel from his knee down and a square piece for a foot.

"Ask your Da would he like to swap," he said, and went and did his rounds.

I had a list of what I wanted to be when I got bigger: a fireman, a soldier, a pilot, a policeman, or a doctor. I crossed soldier off the list.

A few evenings after the ceasefire, Christy inquired, "Tell me, are you good lads? Do you do what your Ma and Da tells you, or are you a handful?"

"Sometimes, mister," the Brother admitted.

21

"Well, 'tis a wonder the Boogie Man hasn't called."

"The wha-?"

"Don't tell me you've never heard of the Boogie Man. Maybe he's called The Sack Man around here."

Me, the Brother, and Kev sat with our gobs open.

"What does he do, mister?" asked our self-appointed spokesman, the Brother.

"It depends," said Christy. "Sometimes, he'll wake you and give a warning, but if you've been really bold, he might put you in his sack and take you away."

I did a wee in my pants.

"Whe… where does he live, mister?" I asked.

"I'm not sure. Sometimes he'll hide behind the curtains, or under your bed. Do you have wardrobes?"

"Ye… ah!"

"That'll be it. That's his favourite hiding place. The wardrobe."

The Brother wasn't too bad. He bravely checked under his bed and behind the curtains, and even peeked into his wardrobe.

Me, I plopped my head onto the soft pillow and pulled the sheets and the pile of old coats Ma used as blankets over my head. My eyes closed. My eyes opened. It was black. I saw his face, as white as snow, peeping out from the wardrobe.

"Ahhh!" I took off, screaming, and headed for safety.

"Shh, pet, what happened? Were you dreaming?"

"I'm scared."

"Scared of what, love?"

"Nothing."

"C'mon, you can sleep between us, but just for tonight."

After a few repeat performances, Da had had enough.

"I'm wandering around the office like a bleeding zombie. What's wrong with that young fella?"

22

A week later, the Brother was brought in as a consultant. After revealing the tale of the Sack Man, Ma threw the teacloth on the table and started.

"Look at me. Look at me, the pair of you. Can't you see I look older than your granny and I'm only thirty-seven? New grey invaders in my hair every morning. Soon, it'll be the colour of the ashes. You've my heart broken, so you have. I'll murder both of you if you go near that fecking building site once more."

Around that time, Ma started washing her hair in the kitchen sink and put stuff in the water to make her hair stay black, and she'd stick curlers in, and when she was finished, she'd wrap a towel around her head. Once, when she took it off, her forehead was all blue and streaky bits ran down her face.

"The Martians have landed," Da said, looking up from the crossword, and Ma looked in the mirror, started crying and took to the bed.

Da made the tea that night. He forgot about the toast under the grill until it went on fire and we'd to go into the back garden to stop coughing and Da said loads of curse words until all the smoke escaped. Then he lit a cigarette and gave us cornflakes instead. And before going to sleep, I knelt and said my prayers, but first, I peeped under the bed, and behind the curtains, and in the wardrobe. Just in case anyone was hiding, waiting to pounce.

Reading, Writing, and Sums

I'd on short khaki trousers, a white shirt, and a hairy jumper Ma knitted. It came down over my knees.

"You'll grow into it in a few weeks," she said before dragging me to "meet all your new friends". Standard brown school bag and open sandals completed the outfit. May 1957, St Agnes primary school in Crumlin. My first day at school.

Ma abandoned me at the gate. I took baby steps into a potholed stony yard, stood with my back to the railings and watched as about a thousand boys ran, screamed, fought, and cried. Someone rang a bell and a nun, about as tall as Da, with a hairy chin, clapped her hands and let out a roar; "All junior infants follow me."

It took her ages to get the last of the whingers over to the corner of the yard where the rest of us stood like sheep. After a second ring of the bell, she announced, "This is Miss McCarthy. She is a newly qualified teacher, so you must behave, and do as you are told, or else you'll have to answer to me."

Miss McCarthy, an angelic young lady with a sensible skirt and a blouse buttoned to the neck, accepted the challenge, and somehow managed to get her flock of eighty-three junior infants into a raggle-taggle line and led us off towards our classroom. She stopped halfway across the yard and pointed to a shed with a rusted corrugated iron roof, about the same size as our coal house.

"Now, boys. Pay attention. This is the toilet. If you need to go, please don't wait till the last second to ask for permission."

Seeing a squadron of flies hovering about the lop-sided door, I decided there and then that I'd be doing all my business at home.

Entering the classroom felt like going into an old church or prison. A shiver ran down my back. I could barely see the ceiling. It was miles away and dark, and I'm sure I saw a bird's nest in a corner where the giant planks met.

Even standing on tippy-toes, none of us could see out the windows. And the place smelt the same as Ma's old slippers. After the last of the cry-babies stopped howling, Miss McCarthy told us to sit anywhere on the lines of benches before she opened a doorstep-sized book.

"I'm going to call out the roll. When your name is called, stand, put your hand up and say 'anseo'. That is Irish for *here*, boys. We'll be learning a lot of Irish soon."

I did as I was told, but the boy sitting next to me had a million freckles and he kept standing and putting up his hand. He did it not once, not twice, but three times, each time giggling and poking me in the ribs.

"This is great gas," he said.

I knew it would be better to have him, whatever his name was, as a friend rather than an enemy.

With the roll call finished, Miss McCarthy handed each of us a square piece of slate, the colour of ash, and a stick of chalk.

"Shhh everybody, sit down and draw a picture."

My education had begun. With the tile resting on my lap, I drew a face. Not sad, but not happy either.

Hands shot up. The toilet message had got through. Some were about to, others were in the process of, and a few finished out in the toilet. But not everyone made it and with the stink in the classroom, I didn't feel like eating my bread and jam when Miss McCarthy told us it was break time. She looked all flustered, with her hair falling into her eyes, and I thought she was going to cry. For break time, Ma had given me two slices of bread and blackberry jam wrapped in greaseproof paper.

Ma and Da picked thousands of blackberries after dragging us along for miles, and then she made jam. Even if it was baking hot, Ma would wear one of Da's old coats down to her ankles so as not to get stung by the nettles. The biggest, juiciest blackas were always high up and Da could pick most of them and Ma, not to be outdone, would reach and let off a string of curses whenever a thorny bramble introduced itself.

Me and the Brother, in our short khakis, could only pick a few. Da didn't want us picking the ones near the ground.

"Leave 'em," he'd say, "I'm sure many a mongrel has cocked his leg along these roads." And we'd spit out whatever we'd picked.

Freckle-Face spat out his sandwich. He showed it to me. His ma had tried to be posh and made a sandwich with slices of tomato, but it had gone all gooey and squishy.

"Gimme a bit of yours, will ya?"

"OK."

He gobbled down the slice in two bites.

"If you gimme some of yours every day, I'll give you sweets," he said and after poking around, took two hairy toffee bonbons from one of his pockets, rubbed them on his pullover and gave me one. I thought it was a good trade. From his other pocket he produced a box of matches and a penknife no bigger than a cigarette. I looked but said nothing as me and matches weren't best friends. Then he mushed up the rest of his sandwich into a ball and rolled it up along the floor.

"My name is Danny Swan. I'm a great fighter."

Miss McCarthy made us put the papers and other rubbish from our lunches into a bin at the top of the room, up by her desk, but one boy skidded on Danny's sandwich ball and walloped his head off the iron leg of a bench and blood gushed onto the floor. It disappeared down through cracks and when Miss McCarthy tried to stop his bleeding and bawling, another boy came in from the yard and he was crying too. He hadn't made it to the toilet and although I couldn't see all the way to the top of the class, I think teacher was crying as well.

When all the commotion died down, she led us out into the yard.

"Now, boys, you can play for ten minutes. Be gentle. No horseplay."

Then she disappeared behind the toilet, and I saw her lighting up a cigarette. Some eejits started calling for their mothers while the rest of us started a game of chase and cops 'n' robbers.

Then we smelt smoke. It was coming from our classroom and Miss McCarthy went doolally, rushing around flapping her hands. The rest of the teachers and nuns came running, and the other classes emptied into the yard. A few minutes later, we heard the clanging bells.

Nobody figured out how it started and although the fire in the wastepaper bin was tiny, the firemen got loads of practice using their hoses. The Gardai were called. The boss nun told everyone to collect their coats and bags and go home early.

My first day at school. After I told Ma everything, she told me to try and sit next to someone else the next day. I don't know what happened, but I never saw Danny Swan again. Maybe he didn't need to go to school after all.

Miss McCarthy arrived one morning lugging two big boxes.

"Now boys. This is so exciting. I'm going to call out your names, and when your name is called, come to the desk and I'll give you two copybooks and write your name on each. You won't have to use the slate anymore."

She did her best to get us started at the Reading, the

Writing, and the Arithme... Arithmet... the Sums. One copybook had boxes. We did sums in that one. The other, with red and blue lines, was for writing. Miss McCarthy lost the run of herself a bit when she started telling us about how words were made up of things called syllables. We hadn't gone beyond – Cat – Mat – Sat – at that stage and the only bills I knew were the ones Da put into a jam-jar until he got paid at the end of the month.

Progress was slow and anyway, it was the nuns who were in charge, and our actual *education* was only number two on their list. Prayers were their business. Prayers first thing in the morning, prayers before the break, prayers after break. The Angelus at midday and more praying before we escaped.

Nuns were called Sisters. Sister Joan, Sister Benedict, and Sister Perpetua all wore black nun's garb, hiding everything except their faces and hands. The boss nun was different. They called her Reverend Mother, but I never saw any of her kids. But that didn't matter. I kept well away because she was a witch. She was the tall one with the dangly hairs on her chin, and she'd a cane, and a witch's hat with a pointed end.

Sister Perpetua, our sergeant major, beat the Ten Commandments into us. We rattled them off like parrots; "Thou shalt not kill, thou shalt not steal, thou shalt not covet thy neighbour's wife." I was OK with the killing and robbing but hadn't a clue what this coveting meant. We did lots of practicing making the sign of the cross and a thing called genuflecting. My knees got sore from all the kneeling and once I got stabbed by a splinter. Ma said it'd be OK in a few days, but it wasn't. It got red and pussy.

"Be brave, son," Da said as he held one of Ma's darning needles under his cigarette lighter. "Must sterilise it, Son." When it cooled down, he poked at my knee until a piece of thorn came out. And I swear I only cried for a minute.

Sister Perpetua told us lots of stories. One was about an angel giving Mary a present of a baby and that there wasn't one God, but three. A Daddy God, a Baby God called Jesus and a Holy Ghost God. She told us she found it hard to follow, but I'd been to see Santa and I'd no problem in believing her fairy stories.

Around that time, after the summer holidays, Miss McCarthy had another surprise for us.

"Tomorrow, we'll be starting with pen and ink."

And next day before calling the roll, she stood at the top of the class looking like a scientist, wearing a blue plastic apron and rubber gloves. Using a wooden spoon, she mixed powder from a bag into a bucket of water. After that, she poured a few drops of the mix into white inkwells that sat waiting on a tray next to the bucket. We'd often wondered what the holes in the tops of the benches were for. Now we knew.

As if carrying a tray of eggs, she made her way along, gently placing an inkwell in every second hole because there wasn't enough for everyone to get one.

Next, she handed each of us a wooden handled dipping pen and with a beaming face told us, "Boys, take great care and dip the nib in the ink and write the letter A in your copybooks."

Doing as instructed, I loaded up the nib, which dropped and splattered across the page. A rub with the back of my hand which I cleaned on my jumper made the mess worse, but I gave it another go and managed a spidery A before feeling something wet at the back of my neck. A genius behind me discovered that by flicking the nib with his fingernail, he could send drops of ink flying everywhere. His discovery was an immediate success and within minutes it looked as if the whole class had come down with measles – blueish ones.

Miss McCarthy got into a right tizzy. Maybe she'd missed the lesson about ink at the training school. On the way out to the yard, I heard her talking to Sister Perpetua.

"I don't know if I can go on. I'm only hanging on by a thread."

After break, we had a visitor. The witch nun. She strode around the room, whishing her cane.

"Now boys, I'm hearing stories, and I don't like what I'm hearing. Would some of you like to come and be in my class?"

In silence, we shook our heads like a troop of monkeys. She held the cane in both hands, bent it almost into a circle and left.

Miss McCarthy didn't cry so much after that.

Follier Uppers

"Can I go to the pictures, Ma?"

She said nothing but looked over at Da, who buried his face in the crossword.

"Please, Ma, lots of the fellas at school are allowed to go all by themselves."

"We'll see. If you get loads of ticks from Miss McCarthy for your homework, we'll talk about it, but you'll have to go with your brother. You're not walking to the Apollo on your own."

"I'm not taking him with me."

Da's face appeared from behind the paper. He said nothing. He didn't have to. A look like that from Da was enough.

I hated doing boring homework, all of them spellings and writing. The sums weren't too bad; I was good at them and knew all my tables.

Agreement was reached and the Brother would bring me on my first trip up to the Apollo in Walkingstown. He never shut up all week talking about the follier upper.

"Ye see, Ma, Roy Rogers an' Trigger were trying to catch up with the steam engine 'cos the driver had an arrow in his belly and couldn't work the brakes or anything and the train was flying along and was coming to a sharp bend and just when Roy was going to jump onto the train... the pictures stopped. That's what always happens. A message comes up on the screen – *To Be Continued,* and that's why I must go on Saturday to see what happens."

He was nearly sweating telling us the story.

I was holding onto my willie, I was so excited.

The pictures started at two, but we struck off at twelve because he said there'd be millions up there.

He was right. The queue was like a long, coloured

31

snake. All boys. Girls could go to other pictures with kissing and dancing and stuff like that if they wanted. The Brother told me not to talk to any of his friends, just stand and do what he told me to do.

When we were at the door, a grumpy man stood and kept shouting, "If I catch any of you lot with bubble gum, you'll get a clatter and I'll feck you out. Understood?"

Janey Mackers, I was holding my willy again.

Two to a seat for sixpence, no matter what size you were. Everyone had penny sweets and toffee bars, but the Brother saw two gurriers standing up on the seats, blowing massive bubbles. They must have been thick because the cranky man spotted them with his torch. He put the torch into a holster thing hanging from his belt, caught the two eejits by the ears and fecked them out.

They turned the lights off, and it was like nighttime when the first picture started. I was still trying to forget all about The Sack Man and hadn't planned on sharing the afternoon with *The Curse of Frankenstein*. I'd hoped Laurel and Hardy would be on.

A man taller than Da and wearing a cloak appeared on the screen. He was in a foggy forest, but I saw his teeth. There were like daggers and dripping with blood and under his arm, he was carrying some fella's head he'd chopped off. I dropped a sweet on the floor and spent a long time down there looking for it, and only resurfaced when the lights came back on.

"Janey Mack, that was brill, wasn't it?" said the Brother.

"Yeah, fantastic," I replied, but I hoped that Mr Frankenstein wouldn't be in my wardrobe that night.

You could buy stuff in between the pictures if you'd any money. Two auld ones, with heavy trays resting on their boobies, walked up and down the aisles selling tubs of ice cream. Nobody we knew ever bought one.

The lights went off again. Audie Murphy was the best fighter in the universe, according to the Brother. Once he'd seen him in a picture called *To Hell and Back*, and after his rifle ran out of bullets, he'd ripped a machine gun off the top of a tank and mowed down thousands of the enemy all by himself.

In this film, he was a cowboy called Walt and because some Indians were nice ones, he was going to help them when some outlaws and greedy people tried to take their land. *Drums Across the River*, it was called. When the enormous battle started, all the Indians were flaking their war drums and all us Indians in the Apollo were whooping and yelping and using the backs of the seats as horses. It was great gas. In the end, Walt and the Indians won.

But then something happened we didn't like. Walt held a lady's hand and went for a walk with her, and then… and then… he kissed her. Everyone was standing again, booing, and waving our fists up at Walt. Loads of hard chaws threw lemonade bottles and ice-cream tubs up at the screen. The lights came on and the crotchety man galloped around like a lunatic giving fellas flakes across the ears for climbing up on the seats and spitting and everything.

When things calmed down, the lights got turned off, and it was time for the follier upper.

"'Tis is the best bit," the Brother said.

The film was jumpy for a while, but it didn't matter. Everyone was standing and shouting as Roy came alongside the train. The engine huffed and puffed out vast clouds and made an awful racket. When Roy jumped on the train, I had to put my fingers in my ears. The clapping and cheering were so loud.

"I knew he'd do it," said the Brother, giving me another elbow in the ribs.

After Roy stopped the train, the cavalry came and chased

away the Indians and saved all the passengers. And in the morning Roy headed for home, but he went a different way and although he was brilliant, he got a bit lost, and a gang of Apache spotted and came after him. Their faces were green and blue and yellow stripes, and some had bows and arrows. Others had guns and I remembered the day Da took me to the pictures, but I wasn't scared anymore. Trigger was faster that all the Indian horses and was getting away, but Roy didn't know there was a massive canyon ahead. He got to the edge and pulled hard on the reins. Looking down, he could see it was deep; he could barely see the bottom.

"No way we gonna get down there, Trigger."

He didn't need to look around. He could hear hooves getting closer and there was no mistaking the war cries.

"What d'ya think, buddy?" Roy said to Trigger, "Only one way outta here. Do ya think you can take the canyon?"

Trigger pawed the ground a few times and then neighed. Roy knew what to do. To get a better run at the canyon, he turned Trigger around and galloped back towards the Indians. Then, as the first arrow went whoosh past his head, he took off his Stenson, gave Trigger a tap on the rear.

"Let's do it, buddy."

Trigger took off, racing so fast, his silvery mane blew flat along his neck. Roy, head tucked in, sat low in the saddle... only a few more strides, and then... and then...

"*To Be Continued.*"

More cursing, screaming, and bottle throwing until the lights went up. We gave our backsides a wallop and me, the Brother, and his gang rode home.

"Ma, Ma, I must go again next week. Wait till I tell you what happened."

I was only halfway through the Roy and Trigger story when she went out the back and tried to squeeze some water from the clothes she'd washed in the sink before hanging tons of our stuff on the line, and she wasn't listening anymore.

I really think that mothers and girls just don't understand about cowboys.

The Star in Crumlin was off limits, even for the Brother. Because corporation houses surrounded it, Ma decided everyone living there were either savages or robbers or a bit of both.

"Don't even dream of going to the pictures down there. Don't you know it's known as *The Rats,* and I'm sure 'tis crawling with fleas?"

But sometimes, the Star got the best pictures before the other cinemas and when the Brother heard *The Magnificent Seven* with the baldy actor, Yul Brynner, was coming, he decided we'd have to do more than dream.

We went.

The queue snaked its way along Kildare Road, and it took ages before we got in. I thought we were lucky because there were rows of almost empty seats under the front of the balcony, but the Brother wouldn't sit in them, and we ended up in the second row from the front.

"Why can't we sit back there?"

"You'll see."

The Three Stooges were on first and when they finished, I took a gawk around because my neck was sore from looking up at the screen. Then I saw why nobody wanted to sit under the balcony. A gang of bowsies up in the front row started chucking all kinds of stuff down on the kids below.

"Look," I said to the Brother.

"I know. I know," he said. "That's why we're stuck here. An' see that fella over in the corner pouring something from that lemonade bottle?"

"Yeah."

"Well, I don't think that's lemonade."

Three or four ushers and usherettes ran around trying the catch the gurriers and it looked like the Battle of Britain with the beams from their torches crisscrossing each other.

Ma was right about The Rats.

Everyone sat down when *The Magnificent Seven* started and it was worth taking the chance because there was loads of shooting and killing.

"What's wrong with your neck?" Da asked when we were kneeling down to say the Rosary after tea.

"Nothing."

"You're the same," he said to the Brother. "The pair of you haven't stopped rubbing and twisting your noggins since you came home from the pictures. What was on in The Apollo, anyway?"

I felt my face go red and that didn't help.

Ma got up and went into the kitchen and when I heard her rummaging in the drawer, I knew we were in for it.

Both of us got two smacks of the wooden spoon, but it was worth it because Me and the Brother got to see *The Magnificent Seven* – no amount of wooden spoon would ever take that away from us.

The Sins

After weeks and weeks of praying, we were ready for First Holy Communion. This meant a new blazer, trousers, and shirt. Everything bought in Cleary's on O'Connell Street. My hands and knees disappeared when I tried on the blazer.

"Ma, it's miles too big. It looks like an overcoat."

"Yerra whisht. You'll grow into it before long."

Yeah, I'd heard that line many a time.

Sister Perpetua took command of preparing us.

"Now boys, it's time to practice for your First Confession and Communion."

She told us lots more about God and Heaven, and it all sounded good, until she terrified us with stories of Hell and roasting in a fire there for eterni... eternit... for a long time.

God, she explained, knew, and saw everything and how He didn't get cross when we broke the rules. But to keep Him happy, and get to Heaven, we'd have to tell our sins to the priest before getting Holy Communion.

"Every time you receive the sacred host, you'll be eating a bit of Jesus."

"Does it taste like a rasher, Sister?" asked Brian, our spokesman.

"Don't be ridiculous, child."

"But Sister, how can we all eat some of Je...?"

"Brian, shut up and sit down."

None the wiser, we left it at that.

As with the praying, we practiced confessions every day, with Sister playing the part of Father Moloney, who called from time to time to check up on us. A man whose football-shaped face always shone, he looked like Friar Tuck except for eyelashes as big as scrubbing brushes.

With Confession Day fast approaching, Sister Perpetua

got more and more addled trying to explain sinning to our mob. Questions were allowed. A big mistake.

"No, Brian, shouting at your brother isn't a sin, but kicking the cat might be."

Hands shot up like rockets. Brian, feeling he was being ignored, stood on his seat with arms outstretched and announced, "Sister, sister, I need to confess. Last night, I pinched my sister's bum. Is that a sin?"

"No, Brian, it's not a nice thing to do, but it's not a sin. Now, sit down and would you stop picking your nose. It's disgusting."

We practiced getting the host hundreds of times. Sister Perpetua broke ice cream wafers into bits and got cross with anyone who stuck their tongue out too far.

"Liam, pull in that yoke. You're like an anteater."

Poor Sister ran out of time and patience; "Boys, with seventy-four of you for Confession, Father Moloney will be extremely busy, so try to keep your list of sins as short as possible."

Perfect. I'd go for one curse and one lie.

Walking in pairs, holding hands, she marched her flock over to the church and brought a few other sisters along to make sure we didn't escape or start acting the maggot.

My turn. With knees knocking, I went into the Confession box and knelt on the step, my head barely reaching the latticed hatch where I'd to confess all my sins to Friar Tuck. Pitch black. I half expected The Sack Man to grab me. When Father Moloney slid open the hatch, all I saw were those bushy eyebrows. With closed eyes I started. "Bless me, Father, for I have sinned."

"Relax, my child. Sure, isn't this your first Confession? Have you any sins to confess?"

"Yes, Father. I cursed once and told a lie."

"Is that all?"

Silence.

I knew God knew everything, but was Father Moloney in on the trick as well?

Tears ran down my cheeks as I blurted, "And I stole a toffee bonbon from the pick 'n mix in Woolworths." It could have been a cough, but I'm sure the lovely man tried not to laugh.

"Well, son, let's forget about that one, but you wouldn't want to make a habit of it, would you? We don't want you growing up to be a robber, do we?"

"Yes, Father, I mean no, Father."

"No matter. For your penance, say three Hail Mary and good luck on your First Communion."

I floated out, made my way to the altar rails and said the prayers, adding in an extra one just in case.

And that was that. No need for Daz or Persil. Three Hail Mary and my soul glistened. If I got a belt of the 53a bus on the way home, it'd be straight up. No worries about burning in Hell for ever and ever.

On the Big Day, Ma fixed a Communion rosette the size of a small cabbage on my blazer before we headed off, and Da had his suit washed and pressed for the occasion. Ma wore a black and white stripy dress and high heels she'd bought especially for the day in the sale in Arnotts.

"They're a bit tight. I'm a 5, but they only had a 4½ left, but I couldn't leave them after me at the price."

She hobbled behind us. I kept looking back at the yellow hat she'd plonked on her head. To me, it looked like a bucket for making sandcastles.

"Not a word," said Da, "but doesn't Ma look like a zebra crossing?"

The church looked as if the circus had arrived, with yellow and white flags hanging from the lampposts and bunting tied to the gates, reaching all the way to the steeple. All the mams and dads gathered for a chat and a smoke while our sergeant major and a posse of teachers corralled and marched seventy-three of us to the top rows of the church. Liam didn't make it. The week before, while whizzing down our road on his bike, he pulled the front brake by mistake and went flying over the handlebars, and instead of his hands, Liam used his face and teeth to stop.

"No more talking or fidgeting," Sister Perpetua ordered.

Father Moloney dressed in his best, said the Mass – in Latin.

Then the big moment. One by one, Sister marshalled us, according to our names, up to the altar rails. Christy Andrews first and Billy Young last. I was in the middle.

After saying a special prayer to Jesus, I stuck out my tongue and Father Moloney gave me my First Communion. Disappointing. It tasted of nothing, certainly not a rasher.

By the time Mass had ended, I couldn't wait to leg it home. No more genuflecting. It was time for collecting. The blazer weighed about a ton, but I couldn't take it off because the neighbours, when I stood outside their gates, mightn't see I'd made my Communion and mightn't have called me in and said: "You look lovely. You're nearly a big boy now."

Most gave me a shilling or a half-crown, but Miss Daly, who lived next door, gave me a ten-bob note. The first one I'd ever owned.

Ma said Miss Daly was loaded because she had sense and never got married or had babies.

By the time I'd finished walking slowly up and down our road, my pockets were bulging. Ma helped me count it.

"You did well," she said. "Almost ten pounds."

A great day. I'd be able to buy millions of gobstoppers and toffee bars, but Ma had other ideas. She snaffled the lot.

"Keep two shillings and I'll put the rest in the Post Office for you."

Not what I'd hoped for. Just as well I didn't know what wrath meant or that it was a sin or my second Confession would have taken much longer.

Mixing with the Big Boys.

After the big day, Da sat me on his knee; "Now, son, although I have my doubts, you have now, according to the Church, reached the age of reason. That means you'll be able to come to the Confraternity Mass with me and your brother." He patted my head, and I knew I was doing something right. He was proud of me. This Mass was a monthly ritual for men of the parish. Real big boy stuff. 9 a.m. in Crumlin for us. Each street in the parish had their own special row in the church, each with a flag showing the street name.

Me, Da and the Brother went early, and I didn't even have to hold Da's hand anymore, and we'd stand outside. Da would chat about football and have a smoke with the other fellas, and I'd look around, and none of the other men ever had their shoes polished like my Da. The Brother wandered about looking for mischief. When we went inside, we'd light candles. I liked that smell, but when we sat in our row, I didn't like the stink because not everyone had a bath on Saturdays, and the place always smelt of pints and farts.

To get Communion, you couldn't eat anything, and had to fast from the night before. If you ate or drank anything, even a few Rice Krispies before taking the host, you were in big trouble. If you died, you'd go straight to Hell. Yep. Eternal damnation for breaking the rules.

This starvation didn't suit me, and on the first morning, I got sick but hung on till Mass finished. On the second and third mornings, I fainted. And because we hadn't stayed till the end of Mass, Da had to go again later because if he didn't, he'd get a black mark on his soul. And Da didn't like going back to the 12 o'clock Mass, because the pubs opened at half past, and he'd be late for his few pints.

My biggest trick was vomiting, fainting, and splitting my noggin all together. I was a child of many talents. Everyone fussed around, and someone went to call for an ambulance, but Da carried me home instead.

Not for the first time, Da had had enough and from then on, we did our own thing when it came to religion.

Medical Science and De Drink.

"I can hardly see you when you turn sideways," Ma said one Saturday after my bath, "and I can count all your ribs." And because I looked as white as the towel, she thought I might die.

She'd take me to a doctor. Mind you, she took her time about it, but after mulling over it for days, she made an appointment. A major move. Doctors, like priests, bank managers, solicitors, and policemen, were best avoided. Either they cost you money or they brought you trouble. Sometimes, if all the saints deserted you, they did both at the same time.

We'd no money to lose and avoided trouble like it was the Devil himself. Inviting the doctor in was quite the gamble.

Dr Wilson, a friendly old guy, known locally as Rudolph with a whiskey-stained moustache, thought I had worms. Instead of medicine, he recommended the occasional bottle of Guinness.

"It'll knock the shit out of the worms and help to build up his muscles," he told Ma before relieving her of a ten-bob note. The Da brought home a bottle from the pub the next night.

"It smells like Mango's wee," I said in protest, but Ma forced two and sometimes three bottles of the black stuff down my throat every week. I hated it.

The Da enjoyed a pint or ten but taking us along usually meant trouble. On the odd occasion we made it to the pub, the order never changed.

"A pint please, a glass of stout for the good lady, a bottle of Guinness for the lad, and an orange for the other boy."

"Why can't I have one of them?" the Brother asked, with a puss like a wet sock.

"'Cos that's medicine for your brother. Now sit down or you won't be getting anything."

Eyes peered over newspapers and little old ladies raised their glasses of sherry in salute when this scrawny thing started sipping his bottle of poison.

"Would you take one look at the young fella with the bottle o' porter, sittin' there like an auld codger? Do you like it, love?"

I'd have the legs crossed, pretending to be enjoying the stuff. "Yeah,'tis lovely."

This drove the Brother mad. The stuff still tasted like Mango's wee, but the look on the Brother's face made it worth the torture.

The Black Babies

Having got the worms sorted out, going blind came next on the list. The school nurse visited and tested everyone's eyes and weeks later, Miss McCarthy gave me a letter to bring home. After reading it, Ma announced, "We've a consultation... with a specialist, no less."

On the other side of Dublin, Me and Ma took two buses and walked miles to get to the clinic for my 11 a.m. appointment. Unfortunately, another four hundred people also had 11 a.m. appointments, and Ma said it made a mockery of the entire process. A barrack-like place with row after row of benches, each one gouged with the initials of previous bored occupants. The putty-coloured paint on the walls was flaking off like scabs and I'm not sure if it was the people or the place, but it all smelt like a dirty dishcloth. I'd never been to a prison, but this infirmary felt like one.

We sat for hours. Ma told me to stop picking my nose, but I was bored. Once, Da said, "If you pick the other end, Son, you'll get bigger bits," but Ma gave out to him. "Don't be so crude."

I picked the sores on my knee for a while and my bum got sore from sitting on the hard bench, but Ma wouldn't let me go wandering around.

"Stay where you are. I don't like the look of some of them in the queue." Luckily, Ma had brought her knitting. She was like lightning with the needles, as good as Zorro with his sword. Many's the time me and the Brother got prodded with the tip of a number 7 or 8.

"Will the pair of ye take your heads out of them comics and do your homework?"

She knitted Aran pullovers with a special type of wool called Bainin. They weighed about four tons because the wool had all the oil from the sheep still in it. And they were waterproof, so we wore them winter and summer, kicking footballs, climbing trees, searching, and finding adventure and sometimes mischief. Ma hated giving them their first wash in the kitchen sink but eventually had to give in when they went the colour of the ashes in the grate. When she lifted them out, as white as flour and smelling of washing powder, she would tell us, "They'll never be the same. All nature's beauty gone down the drain."

I could nearly tell the time, but Ma said it was after 3 o'clock when a nurse with massive boobies and a matching bum led us to see the eye man. He was as wide as the desk he leant against and his head, the size of a bucket, had a mop of raven-coloured spiky hair.

His glasses were as thick as milk bottles, and he was Black. Really Black. He mumbled something in our direction. Ma almost collapsed. Not that Ma was racist – she had had no chance to be. She'd never seen a Black person in the flesh. Neither had I. She had seen them in the pictures and on collection boxes that the nuns told us to fill with our pennies "to save the poor Black Babies".

"Is he really an eye doctor?" Ma whispered to the nurse, "I mean to say, would ye take a look at the specs he's wearing himself?"

She didn't reply but looked Ma up and down as if she had just announced an intention to do a number 2 on the floor. Anyway, the doctor called me by my name and asked if I liked school and playing football. I gave him a "No" and a "Yes". He got me to read letters and numbers before poking and prodding around with all kinds of contraptions. Then he started yabbering. Ma hadn't a clue what he was on about and had to ask the nurse, who looked as if she might explode at any second. Her uniform must have shrunk in the wash.

47

"What's the Blackie mumbling about?"

"A slight squint," was the reply. "The doctor says it should disappear in six months with the help of glasses."

Back home, Ma told Da what happened. "From what I saw today, the Black Babies are doing better than ourselves." Then she emptied the pennies from The Black Baby boxes into her purse and threw the cartons in the dustbin.

The Stiff-Legged Walk

I was six and a quarter when a doctor, with hands the size of shovels, sliced open my stomach and took away my appendix. I didn't miss it because I'd the best time of my life gobbling mountains of sweets. Not penny toffee bars, liquorice bootlaces of clove rock, but real chocolate, like Fry's Cream or Cadbury's Daily Milk. They cost sixpence. That was what we got for pocket money, and it had to last to last the whole week.

Ma spoiled everything when she said I could go back to school.

"Come here till I comb that hair, 'tis all over the place. Here's sixpence. You're to get the bus till you're better. Straight home after school and no hanging around acting the eejit."

"Yes, Ma."

The smell in the kitchen made my mouth water because Ma had made brown bread and packed two slices, slathered with butter and jam, in my schoolbag. She kissed me when I left. I hated that.

"Get the No 52a outside McCarthy's shop, thruppence to school and thruppence home. Walk."

"Ok, Ma."

I galloped or ran all the time because we always played cowboys and Indians, but that morning, I did as Ma told me. My three marbles, a red one, a blue one and a yellow one were in one pocket and I'd a piece of old bubble gum in the other. It didn't taste of anything, but it blew bubbles as big as balloons and I kept it in a matchbox I'd found. Clutching the shiny coin, I turned the corner to McCarthy's...

"Get on."

The Big Brother ambushed me.

"I can't. Ma says I'm to get the bus 'cos of my—"

"Get on or I'll give you a wallop and smash your specs."

I wanted to cry, but he'd have laughed, and anyway, he'd his fist in my jaw, so I hopped on the crossbar, and it hurt a bit.

Halfway up the Long Mile Road, he said, "Get off here."

"But we're not there…"

"Get off. I don't want anyone knowing you're my brother. I'll collect you after school and you're to gimme half the money. We'll get gobstoppers and liquorice in McCarthy's."

After making the Communion, me and the other boys said our goodbyes to Miss McCarthy and the nuns and moved to the big new school up in Drimnagh. Posh it was, with shiny desks and chairs instead of benches. Instead of lady teachers, we now had brothers. Christian Brothers, who swaggered around the place like John Wayne wannabees, looking for any excuse to draw their leather straps like six-shooters from their long black habits and flake anyone they decided had broken the rules.

Ma couldn't figure it out when I wet the bed a few times, and kept reminding me I was a big boy now. Being in the witch nun's class would have been better than this torture house.

I really needed a poo before they released us at three o'clock but hung on. Waiting for the Brother, I knew I'd made a mistake. Bursting to go, I squeezed my bum tight and crossed my legs, then sat on a wall and said three Hail Mary.

But Holy Mary must have been out shopping.

So, I started waddling towards home, khaki shorts, white shirt, and leather school bag dragging. It wasn't pleasant. Poo running down my legs, and into my socks and sandals, all squelchy like.

After ages, the Brother caught up.

"Where were you?" I blurted as tears flowed.

"Playing marbles and I won loads. Ah, jeez, look at you. You've done a shit. You're stinking."

And off with him.

Abandoned, I kept going, every step of the stiff-legged walk a torture, my khakis feeling as if I'd stuffed them with stones. Passers-by gawked before giving me a wide berth.

It got worse when I turned into our estate. Girls were out playing skipping with their rope tied to a gate. Our gate. I soldiered on. The girls stopped singing that stupid rhyme, *Apples and Pears* when they saw me. Some giggled, some moved away, others put their hands to their noses.

You could have heard Ma shouting miles away.

"Jesus wept. How'd you get into this state?"

After dumping me in the bath, she scrubbed with a nail brush, every inch except the appendix scar.

"Ah, Ma, you're hurting me."

And with that, I got a clip around the ear.

"Didn't I give you money for the bus? What happened?"

God forgive me, I confessed.

"I'll murder him," she said. The Brother got the wooden spoon. Worse followed. She took our ill-gotten gains and dropped the sixpence into the special jam jar she kept for emergencies.

"That'll teach the pair of you. Do as you're told and don't be trying to be smart; it doesn't suit you."

No liquorice or gobstoppers that day. Only my ear thumping like a drum.

Every time I touch my scar, I remember that day. I never forgave him, the marble-playing bollocks.

Previously published by Pure Slush Books.

Bells a-Ringing – Again

For once, we did as we were told... well, nearly. Me, the Brother, and the rest of our gang were sitting on the footpath looking at comics, when the Brother got an idea from *The Hotspur*. The comic for big boys, the one with more fighting and blood in it. The Wolf of Kabul, the Brother's hero.

"Look," said he. "We'll build one of these."

The pictures showed loads of kids, all smiling like it was Christmas morning, laughing and racing up and down on weird contraptions.

"They're called go-karts," the Brother informed us. "C'mon, let's get started."

Getting started was a problem. How did you build one? We looked at the pictures a few more times.

"Look, if we get a few planks from Christy, we can make that bit," he said, fierce important like, pointing at the body of the cart, "and we'll get Ma to get an orange box when she goes to the shops, and that'll be our seat. And Da will give us a bit of rope that he has for Ma's clothesline, and that'll be our reins for steering. It'll be great gas. We can have races and everything."

"But what about wheels?" asked my best friend Kevin.

"And I'm not going up near Christy," I said. "I'm not getting me backside walloped."

"Coward," said the Brother as he put his arm around Kevin. "Does your sister still play with her pram?"

"Only sometimes."

"Would she be upset if we took a loan of the wheels?"

Kevin went to negotiate. He came running back a few minutes later, as happy as a dog with ten tails, all ten of them wagging.

"My sister says we can have her pram, but only if we

52

promise to give her loads of spins, and my Ma says we can have the old pram that's in our garage. It's only gathering up dust, she said, and she's never ever, ever going to need it again."

Kevin had three sisters. One of them went to big school and even had a boyfriend who was training to be a mechanic. He wore jeans and my Da said, "That fella's nothing but a bowsie. Jeans are only for ragamuffins and teddy-boys. Look at his long greasy hair. Disgusting."

As Da worked in an office, he was useless at doing jobs around the house for Ma.

"Pen and pencil are my tools," he often said, but he had a hammer, a screwdriver, a hatchet, and a wobbly saw. We used them all, but mostly the hammer. Da called it "The Gentle Persuader". We used it to gently persuade the wheels and axles off the pram.

"Christy will come to work soon. Let's go."

I volunteered to stay behind and be the look-out man.

"Coward," said the Brother again as he took off, with Kevin in tow.

"You'll need nails and screws as well," Christy told the lads. "I'll give you a hand later on."

At teatime, we made our pleas. "Please, Ma, pleeease, I swear to Holy God, we won't go near the houses. Christy won't let us, anyway."

There was no budging her.

"You can go if your father goes as well. I don't want one of you coming back with your fingers hanging off."

"Wha-?" says the Da, putting down the *Evening Press* and lighting up a Gold Flake. "I can't be going up there to your man after what I said about him."

"Sort it out between you," she said, putting away the brown bread and blackberry jam, and starting to do the dishes.

Da let us go on ahead and when he met Christy, he gave him a fag. They talked little, just looked at the ground and kicked at bits and pieces, like horses do when they're hanging around.

"You might like this for your supper," Da said, and gave him an enormous slice of currant bread with lashings of butter.

"Give him that as a peace offering," Ma had said. She was the best baker in the universe.

Kevin's da arrived on the scene and started cursing. He was a great curser, but Da said he was a bit of a gurrier.

"That fella should've stayed where he was reared," Da often said. Kevin's da was a handyman, but Da said he was only a chancer, but he'd loads of tools and thingamajigs.

"The pair of you won't get much fecking building done, standing around like a pair of pricks," he said to Christy and Da. "C'mon, let's make a bleeding start."

Christy got bits of timber, Kev's da measured and hammered and had a pencil stuck behind his ear and a fag hanging from his lip. He coughed and cursed with every second breath. Da did what he was told.

"Would you be able to cut them bits into four pieces, about thirty inches wide?" Christy asked. "We'll fix the axles and wheels to them."

Da was learning, but he didn't like the way Christy was talking to him... like he was an eejit or something.

The sun had gone to bed, and the moon peeped out by the time they had finished. Me, the Brother, and Kev jumped like baby kangaroos, all excited like. Bullet barked and yelped, his tail whizzing around like a propellor. Mango lay stretched out by Christy's fire.

They'd made two carts for us. Big wheels from Kev's pram at the back, and his sister's wheels at the front. Ma had dragged home two orange boxes from McCarthy's and Christy made seats with them.

"Who's going first?" asked Kev's da.

I wanted to, but the Brother pushed me aside. "I'm first. 'Twas my idea."

Kev hopped onboard his chariot and the Brother into his. "I'm only going to give you a small push," Da said. "Remember, there's no brake."

Our road was wide, and Kev's da had a van, but nobody else on our road had a car, so there was no traffic, only sometimes when the builder's lorries came down.

Off they went, and they were flying. The Brother zigzagged from side to side, like a racing driver, steering with the rope that Christy fixed like the reins for a horse. They kept going way beyond our house and I'd to run as fast as I could to keep up.

Then – my turn. My spin wasn't as long as the Brother's, but Da pushed me fast, so fast my hair blew back, and I thought I would take off, and I wanted to stay out till it got dark, but Da said it was time for bed. But we didn't sleep.

Word got around. It always did. Sometimes, we gave it a small push to help it on its way.

Then prams and buggies started disappearing from the other houses and garages, and the sound of hammering and sawing and the occasional unholy oath as hammer met thumbnail could be heard all over our estate. The rest of our gang were building.

One fella's da brought home tiny steel wheels called ball bearings for his cart, and they made a noise like thunder coming at you. Mind you, the eejit thought he was cool but could only go as fast as a caterpillar, so it wasn't even scary.

Ours and Kev's were the best. Ma gave us a faded old cushion to put on our seat, and Kev's sister, the one with the pink hair and the gurrier boyfriend, painted fantastic red streaks along the sides. Like lightning, they were.

Kev's da fixed a bit of wood next to the back wheels. "Try to scrape that along the wheel when you want to stop," he said.

We did. It broke the first time we tried. Instead, we put out our legs and scraped our shoes along the ground to stop, but sometimes we crashed. I'd huge scabs on my knees, but didn't care.

I'm not sure who came up with the idea, but it was Kev's da who made the announcement, roaring as he walked up the road; "Perrystown's Road first Grand Prix next Saturday."

Ma sometimes tried to teach Kev's mother how to cook, but she hadn't a clue and anytime she tried to bake bread or a cake, she made Kev have a taste before his da came home. We got used to hearing "It's like poison", followed by the sound of the dustbin. But she had a sewing machine and could use it. She made a green flag for the starter, a black an' white chequered one for whoever would be at the finish line and lots of smaller flags, all different colours, for the small kids.

Da brought home rolls of the narrow papers bus conductors used in their ticket machines and strung them along between the telegraph poles and tied more to all the gates and the whole place looked like as if a carnival was going on. Kev's da got special thick chalk and marked out the start line up at the top of the road where the new houses were being built and he made the finish line a good bit back from the Stop sign.

Ma never allowed us to go beyond that sign except when going to school. It was like the edge of no-man's-land.

"Don't let me ever catch you sneaking around the corner to McCarthy's shop. There's cars and buses flying up and down."

Me and the Brother did some practice runs during the week after school and I suggested I'd be the driver in the race because he'd be able to push me faster.

"Not a chance. You'll do fine with your long skinny legs."

Ma didn't have a lie-in on race day. Instead, she baked heaps of scones and buttered them while they were still hot and put a dab of her precious blackberry jam on each. As soon as she took the tray outside, neighbours and swarms of their kids descended like a flock of seagulls and Ma ended up having to cut the scones in two, so everyone got a taste. Other mams brought along packets of biscuits, nice ones like Mikado and Jammie Dodgers. Da brought out two bottles of porter, one for himself and one for Kev's da, who looked a howl wearing a span-new pair of white overalls with a rocket transfer stuck on the back. On his head, he'd a German war helmet that came down over his eyes and wobbled every time he moved. Acting the sergeant major, he marched around issuing instructions through a megaphone made from cardboard.

"All competitors to the starting line. Clear the road."

Kev's sister, not the one with the pink hair, the other one with legs like Ma's knitting needles, was the starter.

"Ready, steady," she shouted, dropped the green flag, and we were off.

The Brother was Stirling Moss, and Kev called himself Fangio or something like that. His cousin, who went to big school, pushed him. We didn't think that was fair, but couldn't do anything about it. There were six in the race, but the noisy one with the ball bearings lagged straight away.

When Kev's baby brother crawled out and sat in the middle of the road, a restart was called.

Off we went again. Stirling Moss and Fangio, with big

pram wheels on their carts, battled to take an early lead. By halfway I felt knackered, but terrified to stop, I kept going, my vest clinging to my back.

"Push harder, push harder, will you?" the Brother roared as Kev inched ahead.

By now, everyone living on the road was out cheering and roaring until that stupid dog, Hitler, appeared from nowhere and started yelping and snapping at Kev's cousin's ankles. Da gave him a boot up the ass and that was the last of him.

"I'm going to beat you, I'm going to win!" Kev shouted as we came down the road towards the finish line where his Da stood with the chequered flag. "C'mon Kev, that's my boy. Keep going."

I stopped pushing. Kev's cousin didn't.

The Brother stopped. Fangio didn't.

Well, he did… when he hit the side of the 52a bus.

Kev ended up in smithereens and so did his go-cart. The man from the chemist's shop ran up and stopped Kev's blood leaking and going down the drain before the ambulance men and the fire brigade men and the policemen came screaming along.

Kev was lucky, though. His ma intended to start him at school after the summer holidays, but when he came out of hospital, with a funny-looking face and a weird, stupid smile, she kept him at home for another year.

Da took the hatchet to our cart.

The End of the Month

I'd a loved if Da drove a train or a bus, but he didn't. Because he could do sums in his head, he worked in the office doing adding and subtraction and things like that. He told us he'd to check everybody was honest and not fiddling, and I didn't know what that meant because I thought you'd to have a violin to fiddle. As well as him never having to pay on buses or trains, when we went on our holliers, he got special passes, and we all went for free. First class. Ma would walk along the platform like the bee's knees getting into the posh carriage – and not a bob in her purse. She said some people called it going on vacation, "but they're only posh aul' snobs." To us and everyone we knew, it was the holliers, but, always penniless, most went nowhere.

My Da always wore a suit. And Ma bought shirts with two or three collars. He'd change his collar every few days, and she'd wash and scrub the dirty one with Sunlight soap, and put Robin Starch on it to make it go stiff, and Da would change his shirt again every Sunday morning before going to Mass. Even messing about in the garden digging a place to grow lettuce and onions and spuds, he'd wear his suit. He'd nothing else. Whenever he sweated, off would come the jacket, and he'd roll up the sleeves of his shirt. Then he'd have a fag, not worrying about the massive, yellowish stain under his arms.

And once, we got a few scrawny bits of lettuce, but most of the time the weeds he'd got rid of came back and brought their mates with them.

"He knows as much about gardening as the pair of you know about tidying up the bedroom. I don't know why he doesn't just stick to the crossword," Ma used to say, looking out the window as she ironed the spare collars.

Because Da worked in an office, he got paid at the end of every month, and Ma didn't like that.

"Can't you see his toes are out through the top of the sandals, thanks to those bloody go-carts? He'll have to get a new pair."

"We can't get them this week, Dear. They will have to wait till the end of the month."

"The end of the month, the end of the month, it's always the end of the bloody month," Ma would say, and under her breath, she'd add, "I bet you don't be saying anything about the end of the month to the barman down in The Submarine."

Ma and Da wouldn't talk for days whenever she said something like that.

In December, instead of being paid at the end of the month, Da got paid before Christmas. Brilliant. I remember Santa coming and bringing Cadbury's selection boxes for me and the Brother, and I got a cap gun and a holster, and the Brother got a Meccano set. My mouth watered every time Ma baked for Christmas. She'd mix currants, and raisins and sultanas and cherries and other stuff in a gigantic bowl. Me and the Brother would grab two or three cherries when she wouldn't be looking and get a tap of the mixing spoon whenever she caught us. She baked two cakes, one for us and one for her brother Eddie, who lived on his own on a farm down the country somewhere. Ma left us to lick the bowl and the wooden spoon after she'd put the cake in the oven, and the smell got even better when she made us scones or bread with currants. The puddings and cakes got a good lash of whiskey and sometimes a drop of something else that Da called "de craythur". He had a bottle of this stuff he got from a man at work, wrapped in an old *Evening Press*, hidden at the back of his and Ma's wardrobe. The Brother found it one day when he went rummaging while Ma was doing the shopping.

"Pooh! What's that stink?" I asked, jumping back. I half expected The Sack Man to leap out.

"That's only the smell of mothballs, you eejit," the Brother said. "Moths don't like bread and butter and jam. They eat socks, underpants, and jumpers instead, but the mothballs kill 'em. Here, try one. It tastes like a gobstopper."

But I wasn't *that* big an eejit.

In at the back, he found a lemonade bottle. "I'm gonna take a slug," he said. And he did. A big mouthful. Then his eyes started flying around and went all watery like he was crying, but he wasn't. He screamed and jumped around like Geronimo doing a war-dance.

"My stomach, my stomach, my belly's on fire," he shouted. I started laughing. He gave me a wallop. Then Ma came home, and I didn't know what to do.

She made the Brother stick his fingers down his throat until he got sick and when some of it missed the toilet, she gave him a slap and made him drink hundreds of cups of water.

"Honest to God," she said, "I can't even go to the shops. You've me heart broken. I feel like drinking the rest of that poteen myself. Not a word to your father. He'd murder the pair of you."

After Christmas, when we'd eaten all the turkey, ham, cake, pudding, sweets, and lemonade, and when all Da's bottles of stout and Ma's sherry were gone, January arrived. Ma's purse was full of change, pennies, and shillings, but only a few pound notes. Da's pockets were empty.

Da made our own bog paper in January. Using a ruler and a special sharp knife that me and the Brother could never use, he would cut squares, 4 inches by 4 from the *Sunday Independent*. Da was precise in things like that. He enjoyed using the pages with pictures of the men who were supposed to be running the country – "Fecking gobshites" he called them. He made holes in the corners with a punch he brought home from work and after feeding square after square onto a bit of wire from a coat hanger, he'd hang his creation from a nail banged into the wall next to the loo.

I never liked this paper. When you wiped your bum, it'd go skeeting up your back and my hands got all black from the ink. Ma used to hide a proper toilet roll in her handbag and minded it like a lump of gold.

And because she had no money, Ma cooked different things for the dinner. My Da hated chips, but Ma and me and the Brother loved them. Ma made the best ones in Ireland. After peeling and chopping the spuds, she threw them in a basin of water. Then, after drying them on a tea cloth, she'd cook them in dripping and put on lashings of salt and vinegar and we'd eat thousands of them. Da preferred spuds. Spuds in their jackets.

"A meal in itself," he'd say. "A good pinch of salt, a knob of butter, and you're away for slates. I read somewhere that if you ate nothing else but spuds, you'd survive."

He'd spend ages mashing up mine, sometimes making a shape like a battleship with bits of sausage sticking up like funnels. Or else he'd make an aeroplane shape with wings and everything and I'd gobble up the lot.

Things were different in January. The first week, we'd have chips, rashers, sausages, and eggs every day. Second week, we'd have chips, sausages, and eggs. And in the third week, it was chips and eggs. For the last few days, we survived on chips, chips, and more chips.

Then the big day came. We'd get the smell of frying from down the road. In the pan, millions of bits of onion sizzled away, and a huge steak, so big it dangled over the side. In a pot, a load of floury Golden Wonder popped outta their skins. Da had come home early from doing his sums and sharpened his knife on a special stone and readied himself.

Ma took four plates from the oven, and me and the Brother weren't even fighting. Da had the steak and all the onions on his plate and cut an enormous piece the size of my hand and put in on Ma's plate. Then he cut two long slices. They were like rulers and gave one to me and one to the Brother. Even Mango got a taste, a small fatty bit... 31st January – pay day – always tasted of steak.

Three in the Bed

"Mango has his own gang of friends," Ma told me, "and he plays with them at night when we're asleep. That's why we leave the kitchen window open, so he can come in and out as he wants."

And we never locked our back door because there was always one neighbour coming around, looking for "a drop of milk till I go to the shop". Sometimes, Kev's ma asked Ma for a half-crown, but Ma never gave her money.

"I'm sure that one is on the sherry."

Sometimes Da's boss sent him down the country to do his sums, checking and making sure no one was robbing down there. Ma didn't like when he went away. Me and the Brother loved it though because he'd always bring back chocolate and sweets. Real chocolate, like Fruit & Nut and Tiffin, and Scots Clan sweets, not like the penny toffee bars we'd get in McCarthy's. Ma always got a Cadbury's Walnut Whirl.

Once, I stuffed a whole lump of toffee in my mouth, and it got stuck and when I poked at it with a pencil, my tooth in the front came out as well.

"You look a right sight, so you do," Ma said, and the tooth fairy never came that night.

With Da down in Cork and Limerick for a full week, Ma promised us a treat for tea on the Wednesday.

"Who'd like drop scones with Golden Syrup?"

Me and the Brother shouted so loud Mango woke, stretched, and miaowed. As Ma mixed flour, sugar, eggs and a pinch of salt, the Angelus bells started clanging on the radio and went on and on and on. Six o'clock. We blessed ourselves and pretended to say our prayers. The Brother stuck his tongue out, trying to make me laugh, but when the news came on Ma told us to "shh."

"This is Radio Eireann. The news headlines. A convicted murderer has escaped from the Central Mental Hospital. Gardai advise this man is extremely violent and should not be approached. People are asked not to go out after dark and to secure their homes and business premises."

"What does all that mean, Ma?" asked the Brother as the first of the scones hit the roasting hot frying pan.

"Nothing. Let me alone while I get these finished, and we'll have to eat them quickly. I want to get tidied up in here."

"But it's not even dark outside, Ma."

"Do as you're told."

When we'd gobbled all the yummies, we'd to wash our faces and put on our jammies. Then Ma called us back into the kitchen. "Come here, and help me push the table over behind the door."

"Why are you doing that, Ma?"

"No why. I'm going to wash the floor later, that's why. Now hop up there and close that window."

"What about Mango?"

"To hell with... he'll be fine. He'll just have to stay with one of his friends."

Every Saturday morning, me and the Brother were allowed into Ma and Da's bed and Da would read our comics, but this was only Wednesday and Ma said, "You can sleep in my bed for tonight." We loved that, and Ma told us stories about growing up in the country and all about milking a cow and she would show us when we went on our holliers.

In the morning, she wouldn't let us go to school on our own and came with us. "Ah, Ma, we look like right sissies," said the Brother, but she marched on, looking left and right in case the loony hopped out from the neighbour's hedge.

And every night after that while the Mad Man ran loose, Ma kept washing the kitchen floor and pushing the table up against the door. We didn't see Mango for days. Ma told us more stories, and we cuddled up together, but I couldn't sleep because she said we'd leave the lights on "Just in case one of you needs to do a wee".

Friday morning – *"This is Radio Eireann. Good morning. The news headlines at 8 a.m.. Gardai have confirmed that they found the escaped prisoner dead during the night. Apparently, he had been trying to climb the perimeter wall into the hospital."*

"Thanks be to Jesus."

It was the first time I'd ever heard Ma curse.

"Just shows ye, doesn't it? The poor fella must've seen what it's like living around here and felt safer inside."

Then she opened the kitchen window, gave us hugs, and we galloped off to school.

Part 2

Heading West

Heading West

August 1959

"Where's the toilet, Da?"

He took a drag of his Gold Flake and put an arm around my shoulder.

"Son, finish your porridge and I'll show you."

I wolfed down the last few spoonsful and Da, stooping as we went out, led the way to the back of a cottage, where scrawny weeds lived among stones and gravel. Standing there, arms outstretched, palms upturned, he reminded me of Moses, the holy man.

"Son, this is where you do your business."

"What do you mean, Da?"

"Well, you might not have noticed, but Uncle's house doesn't have a sink or taps. That's because there's no running water, and therefore there is no toilet. I'll go to the well later to fetch water, but there you are now. You've got the entire countryside to choose from."

And with that, he left, but not before giving me four squares of loo paper – made from newspaper and brought all the way from Dublin.

All I saw for miles were funny-shaped fields of nettles and thistles, which could inflict life-threatening injuries to my bum, but I'd no choice.

We were on our holliers at Uncle Eddie's cottage. Ma said we'd been there when I was in nappies, but I was big now, nearly seven and a half.

We all had a bath the night before we left Dublin, and it wasn't even a Saturday. Me and the Brother first and when Ma finished scrubbing the dirt off us, she washed, dried, and combed our hair. Then we put on our jammies, and Da read us stories from *The Beano* and *The Hotspur*.

The Brother could read, and I nearly could, but the stories were better when Da read them.

Ma boiled a kettle, poured the water into the bath, and locked the door. When she came out, wrapped in a massive towel, she looked stupid with those roller things in her hair. Then it was Da's turn. He didn't bother getting more boiling water and hopped in. Ma sat next to us and cut her toenails.

In the morning after finishing our porridge, Da made sure everyone went to the toilet before we headed off, all dolled up, for the train station. We left much earlier than when we went to school, and I yawned most of the way on the bus. Da wore his best suit, charcoal grey it was, and didn't show the stains, a shirt the colour of a duck's egg, and a blue tie. He never owned a jumper, and as for jeans, "Jeans are only for gurriers and teddy-boys."

Ma smelled nice. She'd on a fresh dress with tulips and roses, all different colours, like the wallpaper in the good room. This was where she took the priest when he called once or twice a year, looking for money. She'd give him tea and a half-crown, but sometimes if it was near the end of the month, Ma didn't open the door and we all hid in the kitchen.

On the train, we plonked ourselves in a compartment, first class, of course, and closed the sliding door so no one else could get in. Da pulled the leather strap and lowered the window, and I'd my head stuck out even before the man waved his green flag. The Brother stood in the corridor, half hanging out a window he'd opened by himself.

"Dear Jesus, Son," Da said, dragging him back, "Do you want to spoil the holidays before they begin?"

We left the smoke and millions of TV aerials behind us and trundled on, clickety-clack, clickety-clack. After a few miles, with nothing to see but fields, cows, and sheep, Ma got me to practice my spelling by calling out the names of the stations that we'd be stopping at.

"Try this one," she said as the wheels screeched when the driver put on the brakes. I put my hands to my ears because I hated that noise. Like when Miss McCarthy dragged the chalk across the blackboard. It made my teeth go funny. I rattled off the letters; T-u-l-l-a-m-o-r-e. Ma said I did well. Then we had tea from a flask and ham sandwiches with the crusts on.

We got off at a place with a funny name, and Ma and Da started laughing. Dead flies and soot were stuck to my clinic issue specs. And when Ma took them off to clean them, she said I looked like Al Jolson, whoever he was.

"Ah Jeez, if only we'd a camera."

Da went looking for a man with a car and found him. He'd one leg longer than the other, and we piled our luggage into his car and chugged along bumpy, windy roads and I got sick. The man got cross and Da cursed.

After ages, I needed a wee.

"Can't you not hold on, child?"

"Nah, I'm bursting."

By now we were on a long, narrow but straight road that went through the biggest bog in the country, or so Da told us.

We stopped.

"Hurry on, Son, don't take all day."

Da stood next to me, but being a big boy, I took two more steps up the road.

"Dear God, can't you just do your wee where you are?"

I got out my willie and took one more step… and fell into a bog hole. You could've heard Da cursing back in Dublin. He pulled me out; Soaked to my ears I was. And it stank. Ma got out and after drying me and changing my clothes, we climbed onboard again and the man with the short leg got cranky. The Brother pinched me and Da lit a fag.

But I still needed a wee and we'd to stop again. Da left off another string of curses and the man revved the engine and it nearly went dark from all the fumes.

The moon had pushed the sun to one side by the time the taxi swung off the tarred road and crawled down a stony boreen where grass tickled the car's belly.

"Buses, train, change trains, another train, and a taxi. I'm sure Hannibal's' crossing of the Alps was easier than this ordeal," Da said, lighting up another cigarette before paying the man.

Waiting for us, sprawled out, legs dangling from the backboard of a donkey and cart, was Ma's brother. My uncle Eddie. A Woodbine in one hand, the other buried deep, scratching something.

"You're here, I see."

He hugged and threw me way up, nearly as far as the clouds. My Da reached the clouds almost, and Ma said it was as well because he spent most of his time floating around up there. Eddie didn't. Instead, he'd grown sideways with a tummy like Billy Bunter and a bald head that shone as if he'd polished it.

All aboard, we headed up the boreen, the cart rocking from side to side. The donkey looked tired, needed a bath, and wasn't in a hurry.

"What's his name?" my Brother asked.

Eddie laughed. "He's a she. This is Wonkee. We'll take it easy with her," he said, looking down at a gammy hoof. "She's got a bit of a delay in that one."

He let me hold the reins, and the Brother didn't appreciate that.

Yep, I'd arrived in cowboy country. I kept an eye out in case Geronimo or any of his braves attacked. A long way from the chimneys and television aerials of Dublin to Elphin, county Roscommon. I jumped when two wolf-like creatures, eyes wide, appeared. Horrible hairy things. They ran as outriders, barking, showing off sharp, sparkling teeth.

"Say hello to Rainbow and Buttercup."

Dogs blacker than the crows that flew above us. I never figured out that one, but we became best friends.

The cottage, white, long, and narrow, stood out like a shoebox, almost surrounded by bushes and trees where the birds lived.

"You gave the place a lick of paint, Eddie," Ma said.

"Sure, I had to what with all you important people coming."

"What's that on the roof, Da?"

"That's called thatch, Son. It's made from a special grass. Someday, Eddie will show you how it's prepared."

"Don't think it'd be much good, Da, if the Apache use flaming arrows."

He gave me a funny look. A worried one.

We unloaded our bags, and Eddie pushed the door. It had two parts. The top swung open, but the bottom needed a kick.

"Don't you have a key?" I asked.

Uncle Eddie's laugh came from his belly and sent an echo bouncing across the stony yard.

"Key? What would I be doing locking anything? The only thing roaming around here is the fox."

It was dark inside. An inky, damp dirt floor smelt of smoke and cats' wee. I hoped Kev would remember to feed Mango. At the far end, an open stone fireplace, black as tar, with pots, pans and kettles scattered about the grate. An army of turf stood to attention on each side, and I was sure a witch lived there once. Eddie switched on a light, but it

72

made little difference. Along one side, I saw a long table and two benches. All wobbly, and I think Uncle had built them. A picture of Holy God hung on the wall, but I couldn't see Him properly. Soot covered everything.

"This is the kitchen," said Ma. "Come on, I'll show you the rest."

Two rooms. One was Eddie's, so small we couldn't all fit in together. Over a single metal bed, piled high with well-worn coats, hung a faded picture of The Sacred Heart. In the corner, a dresser. A paint tin acted as a substitute for a missing leg. A window the size of a biscuit tin made sure the place wasn't ever going to be drowned by sunlight. The other room was the same, except it had a double bed for Ma and Da.

"Where are we sleeping?" asked the Brother.

"The pair of you will sleep up there," she said.

In the corner, above the Holy picture, a ladder created from bits of wood led up to a cubbyhole.

"It'll be like a camp or a fort in the cowboys, Da. I'll be the sentry," said the Brother, scampering up the six rungs. Da went next. The ladder wobbled. I followed. It swayed some more and creaked, and I knew if it collapsed, I'd get clobbered, but we made it. A mattress and two blankets filled the floor.

When bedtime came, I said my prayers, but couldn't sleep. I didn't fancy the look of the thatch. Long dangly bits of straw stuff and monster spiders' webs dangled down. I wasn't afraid of spidery things, but wondered what else lived up there waiting to pounce after I closed my eyes.

Meeting the Ladies

After I'd done my business, Da, puffing away, headed down through misshapen fields to fetch water, an enamel bucket in each hand. He wore his suit, but no tie. Da never owned a t-shirt or a jumper.

"C'mon you," Ma said. "It's time you met the ladies."

"What, girls? I don't like girls, Ma."

"Come on."

Outside, across a stony, weedy patch, stood two sheds, made of rock and stone with rusted roofs. They and the ivy clinging to the walls had got a lick of paint as well, but Eddie must've run out of whitewash. They looked sad and ready to fall.

"What's in there, Ma?"

"Open the door and see for yourself."

The rickety door squealed when I yanked it and peeked inside. Cobwebs dangled from the ceiling, and I expected someone or something to reach down and grab me.

"Go on in, will you?"

The place was full of hens or ducks clucking away, each one plonked on its own straw bed. Ma whooshed them and they scattered, shrieking, feathers and hay mixing with the musty air.

"Look Ma. Eggs, real eggs."

"Don't be gawking at them. Collect them."

Keeping an eye on the owners who still flustered about, I took baby-steps, stood on tippy-toes, and collected my first, warm golden nugget. We got six. I carried one, and Ma cradled the rest in her apron. And when I sneezed, the whole flock went loopy again.

"You can gather them from now on. The hens lay once a day, sometimes twice, if they're in a good mood."

They performed well for my initial visit, but after that,

went on strike. After a few barren days, Ma revealed that going into the coop every twenty minutes and rustling them from their nests wasn't helping with productivity.

Da returned, shirt clinging to his belly, and took off his jacket and wellies. He put on his shiny black shoes, lit a fag, and headed out with six squares of paper.

"Ma, Da must have a big bit of business to do."

She laughed, but Da was back in a flash, eyes bulging, walking in his socks, holding his shoes out in front.

"Are you thick or something, child? When I told you to go anywhere, I didn't mean you to go at the gable end of the cottage!"

After he'd cooled down, he used grass, bits of stick and the buckets of water to clean his brogues. Then he put on his wellies and headed off back to the well. I went with him. Down through fields with more thistles, some as big as me. Da carried the buckets, and I'd a little one.

"This is it, son. This is where we get our water."

I looked. I looked again, peering at this manky deep hole in the ground surrounded by barrels half buried in muck. A few cows were drinking and swishing their tails to keep the millions of flies away, but they skedaddled when they saw us coming.

"We can't drink that stuff, Da. It must be poison."

But Da wasn't in the humour for a debate.

"Dear Jesus, Son, just hold this bucket while I lower and fill this one."

Using a long rope with a hook at the end, he dropped the bucket, and it disappeared off down the black hole. I did my best, but when the flies started buzzing around my head, I'd no tail to shoo them away, and my wellies squelched and got stuck and I fell. After Da cursed, I started crying. Tears ran down my hot face into the bucket, but I don't think any snots went in. He gave me a piggyback, and we

75

only got one bucketful and lots of that splashed out on the way back up the hill to the cottage.

"Look at the state of you," said Ma.

Da sighed and went for a walk and Ma took my hand and said, "C'mon, let's introduce you to Deirdre."

"Who?"

"Deirdre. She's like one of the family."

Standing in a shed, the one next to the hens, stood Deirdre. A cow. A massive black one, as big as a baby elephant. With treacle-coloured eyes, she looked me up and down before releasing a long moooooo which rattled the tinny roof, and I grabbed my pants to stop me from doing a wee.

I wasn't sure if I liked her, or, more importantly if she was fond of me.

Ma carried a bucket and in the corner sat a tiny stool with three legs.

"Pass me that," she said. "Deirdre should've been milked hours ago."

Ma plonked herself on the milking seat right under the cow's belly, which was bigger than any balloon I'd ever seen, and pulled at four gangly bits. They were like willies. And then, as if by magic, milk squirted into the bucket.

"Want a taste?" Ma said, and before I could answer, she spattered milk all over my face… and it was hot.

"Do you want to try?"

I took a step backwards.

"Maybe next time."

With the pail filled, we headed back across the yard and Ma used her free hand to scoop out bits of straw and tiny specks of dirt that floated to the top. Inside, she covered the bucket with a tea towel before putting it over in the darkest corner, away from the fire.

"That'll keep out the flies and any other visitors," she said.

After a few days of watching, I helped with the milking. They weren't willies, Ma told me.

"They're called teats."

Although a hefty creature, Deirdre didn't frighten me. Placid is how Ma described her. Liquorice wasn't.

"A right cranky bitch, this one," was how Ma described *her*, dragging a reluctant goat into the shed. I thought only men had beards, but she had one, black and grey it was, and she'd poo sticking to the hairy bits around her bum. Our dustbin stank and so did she. She had to be milked every day as well, and had two teats, but anytime anyone went near, she lashed out with horns as sharp as spears. So I left Ma to do that job.

Liquorice wasn't fussy. She ate everything. Nobody figured out how she reached them, but once, she pulled a pair of Da's underpants from the clothesline and took off, with Ma running after her, waving the sweeping brush. Liquorice won.

"The stupid eejit must've been starving to eat them," Ma said, sweat pouring down her face after the chase.

The Shopping

With Wonkee at retiring age and as Eddie only had one bike, my Da had a dilemma. He'd said they both needed to go shopping every night after the tea.

"The four-mile walk to Elphin isn't a problem, but the return journey could be a different story."

Eddie and Da laughed and Ma threw her eyes to Heaven. I couldn't understand why Eddie couldn't go on his own, but the two of them struck off. Da on the crossbar, his telegraph pole legs sticking out, and Eddie, his face getting redder by the second, doing the pedalling.

One morning, Da didn't get up for breakfast, and when he did, he had cuts on his face, and a hole as big as a potato in the knee of his trousers and I saw blood. Maybe he had been in a boxing match. And lost.

"What happened, Da?"

"Turbulence, Son. We hit turbulence on the way home."

"What's that, Da?" But before he could answer, Ma gave him a look, and he said no more and went outside.

Hearing whistling and singing, I ran, sucking a red and white spearmint drop, and saw Eddie coming up the lane with the bike over his shoulder. He looked as fresh as the taste of the sweet except for the zigzag scrape on his noggin.

It took him until teatime, using thingamajigs and spanners to fix the bockety wheel and straighten the handlebars, and when he'd finished his boiled egg, he headed off. Da didn't. Instead, he sat at the table with a deck of cards playing patience, smoking fags, and trying to talk to Ma. She gave him the look.

Ma had no cooker. She cooked and baked on the open fire.

"All over a hundred years old, made of iron," Da told

us, pointing at the menagerie of pots and pans hanging from a yoke he called a crane. The frying pan was as wide as the barrel outside. The one Ma collected rainwater in.

"The purest water you'll ever wash your face with."

She baked every morning. After mixing brown and white flour, she poured in sour milk and a pinch of salt, patted the loaf into a round shape and threw a handful of porridge oats on top. Her creation went into a pot with a heavy lid called a bastable and pushed it in among glowing sods of turf.

"I'm after singeing my hair and eyebrows again," she cried many a time after finishing the manoeuvre. "I must look like a traveller. God knows, I've no need for any war paint or lipstick up here keeping all your bellies filled."

The bread had a crunch and a springy softness inside. While still hot, Ma spread an unhealthy amount of butter on slice after slice. Me and the Brother ate tons of it. Better than any sweets or chocolate.

"You lot don't know how lucky you are, better fed than gamecocks, so you are."

And once, Da woke us early, before the sun had time to dry the silvery sheen from the grass.

"C'mon, I made a discovery when out doing my business."

We threw on our clothes and wellies and, with sleep in our eyes, struck off. Da lifted me through a gap packed with muck, cow shit and flies and then we saw them. Mushrooms. Millions of them.

"A present from the gods," he said. "Now, stop staring and start picking."

It didn't take us long before we had filled two buckets till they overflowed. Back home, Da, using a poker as long as himself, encouraged four of five sods of glowing turf to the edge of the hearth and let them rest. Ma busied herself plucking out the stalks and chucked them into a nearby skillet.

"They'll not be wasted. We'll make soup with them tomorrow."

After she'd put a knob of butter and a pinch of salt into each one, Da took over. He lay the mushrooms, one by one, in military formation on the dusky grey sods. Then we watched and waited. It didn't take long before they turned the colour of marmalade with a bubbling puddle in the centre.

Ma explained. "That's the butter, salt and the juices, all mixing."

Then, as if handling sticks of dynamite, Da lifted each one with the tongs and placed them on a plate to cool. Ma took a still warm loaf and slathered each slice with butter. And then we feasted. My favourite part was the salty, buttery juice.

Keeping the Cool

Deirdre's milk went yucky after about a day, and even Da didn't like it in his porridge.

"I'd love to get a fridge sometime," Ma said.

We didn't have one in our house back in Dublin. In Summer, Ma kept bottles of milk and butter in a bucket of water under the sink.

"I hear Ned and May down at the cross got one of them fridge things," Eddie said.

"What?" said Ma, dropping the tea towel.

"'Tis true. Dollars came from America to your man, Brennan, in town. Brennan with the hardware shop. You remember him, surely?"

"I do. I do. Didn't I learn the reading and writing in the same school as him? A cute little weasel with a face like a hen's arse."

"And he hasn't changed. I'm told the money arrived with instructions for one of them fridge contraptions to be delivered as soon as the electricity came their way. They got connected a few months ago, but I don't think they want the bother or have much truck with it. Some people are scared of it, thinking it'll set the house on fire."

"A fridge. A fridge in Ned and May's. I don't believe it. A few bars of carbolic soap would be more in their line. Do they ever give themselves a rub of a sponge or are they afraid of water or something?"

"Why don't we take a wander down after the tea and you can see for yourself? She'd love to see you. Sure, it must be years since you saw her."

After we milked Deirdre and Liquorice, and finished our bread and jam, the lot of us struck off to investigate, down our boreen and past the well. Buttercup and Rainbow raced ahead, chasing anything that moved. At the bottom, we turned left and headed down a narrower lane with so many twists and turns, I nearly got dizzy.

Ma issued instructions, a finger wagging in case we weren't listening.

"Now! Listen, the pair of you. Don't just stand gaping at it and mind your manners."

The cottage, with weeds growing on the thatched roof, never enjoyed a splash of whitewash.

"God bless all inside," Eddie said, poking his red nose in the door.

The place smelt worse than Liquorice. A man wearing a flat cap which, like himself, looked a hundred years old, sat stooped under the chimney, taking long draws from a pipe which sent clouds of smoke to join wisps coming from a sad-looking fire. He didn't stir or speak but beckoned us in with a wave of what looked like a blackthorn stick. A lady, wrapped in a black shawl, sat alongside.

She's definitely a witch, I thought. A small one. She sat, saying her prayers, a lengthy Rosary dangling from her lap.

"Will you look who's here? The lads all the way from Dublin. 'Tis great to see you," she croaked.

"We were just going for a stroll, May, and said we'd drop in and say hello."

"Well! Come up to the fire till I get a decent look at ye. And who are these two fine buckoes? Will ye have tea, or maybe something stronger?"

"Thanks, May, but sure we're only now after finishing the supper."

Uncle Eddie must've been thirsty.

"Maybe a small one. You always have a good bottle stashed away, Ned."

It took Ned an age to get going, relying on the stick to limp over and open, probably for the first time in years, the dresser. The door squeaked at being disturbed. After foostering about, he emerged with a bottle and three glasses. He half blew, half spat into each before filling them almost to the top. One for Eddie, one for Da, and one for himself. Ned left the cane behind and waddled back to his throne.

"Slainte," they said, and drew big sips.

Ma gave Da a dirty look.

The only spattering of light came from the miserable fire, but we couldn't miss it. Plonked in the middle of the floor stood a fridge.

Eddie spoke. "How're ye getting on with the fridge?"

Ned took another pull on the pipe and disappeared in a cloud of smoke.

"'Tis handy," he said.

"It must be great, May, for the milk and butter, and the meat?" Ma inquired.

"Yera, not at all. Haven't we done fine for nearly eighty years without that gadget cluttering up the place, but himself finds it useful?"

"Aye," Ned said, "take a look."

The Brother sprang, opened the door, and reported; "A box of ear-tags, a ball of twine, scissors, and scraps of paper."

The flex and plug lay on the floor – homeless.

Knowing Your Bullocks

Bullocks! Bullocks! It's OK to say bullocks. It's not a curse. I'd heard Eddie and Da talking about bullocks.

"It's quite simple, Son. Bullocks and heifers are all cattle, kind of baby ones. Bullocks are the boys and heifers are the girls."

Problem solved; I knew my bullocks.

"Eddie buys baby calves, and they eat any grass they can find and when they grow up, he sells them to another farmer who gives them heaps more fodder until they get huge, and he sells them to the butcher. Then we eat them."

I didn't understand that bit, but I nodded anyway.

"Fair day is Friday," Eddie announced, giving his head a rub to freshen up the shine.

"I'll be taking five to market and could do with an extra pair of hands."

"Can I come, can I come?" me and the Brother roared.

"Shhh, will you? It's not that easy," Da said. "We'll be walking the four miles into Elphin."

"And we'll be walking home again if the price isn't right," Eddie added, "and we'll be heading off before dawn to get a good spot to do the deal."

We took no notice. We were going.

Come Friday, Ma had us up before the cock started crowing and, after washing our faces, forced us to eat massive bowls of porridge and do our business. And she'd cut big thick slices of bread and made rasher sandwiches.

Off we headed, the Brother leading the way with Buttercup and Rainbow on either side. Me and Da took up the rear. Eddie reached and cut two sprigs, each the length and thickness of a brush handle.

"Give 'em a flake of these if they wander off."

84

Although perished with the cold, we were cowboys on roundup and giddy with excitement.

I'd never seen so many stars up in the black sky trying to show off.

"There must be millions of them, Da."

"Probably."

Then he pointed out the important ones, the North Star and The Plough, before they went to sleep with the moon. The bullocks must've eaten a lot for their breakfast because there was cow shite everywhere and I nearly skidded in it a few times, and it took *hours* to get to Elphin.

The morning, when it came, wasn't as nice as the night before and a mist fell when we arrived. The place was a mad mixture of men and cattle as echoes bounced around the dim, foggy street. Thousands of bullocks stood shitting or pissing, and a greeny brown river flowed.

"That's called slurry," Da told us.

Farmers shouted and flaked at their animals, trying to shoo them into little pens which stretched the length of the town. Most did what they were told, but a few, overcome by the excitement of the day, took off lowing and mooing, followed by the farmer waving his stick and cursing his head off.

Eddie drove our five away up town.

"The stalls are like corrals in the cowboy pictures, aren't they?"

"Sure are, pardner," Eddie replied, "but 'tis fierce important to get the sweet spot to catch the eye of them that'll be buying."

Satisfied he'd done well, he gave the man in charge two shillings.

"I'll take a wander and see who's buying."

This left me, the Brother and Da, wearing his suit, in charge.

Cold damp steam came off the backs of our bullocks and their soft musty breath had a funny smell, but I liked it.

With my wellies feeling as heavy as lead, I dragged my feet until Da told us to sit outside the chemist shop and we gobbled our sandwiches, even the crusts, but we gave Buttercup and Rainbow a taste. Eddie came back and gave each of us a bag of bonbons and we took off.

All the shops had barricades in case any bullocks tried to go shopping, but the footpath was full of stalls selling all kinds of things: delph, old clothes, spanners, one was selling chickens and baby turkeys.

Da said, "You'd find everything from a needle to an anchor around here if you wanted one."

Up by the church, a man sat on a milking stool, surrounded by pots, jugs, and buckets, and we watched as he bent, tapped, hammered, and rolled sheets of tin into shape. He finished a saucepan while we were there and then he took a long, thin piece and made a tin whistle. It was like magic.

He gave the whistle to a girl who played a tune and danced at the same time. About the same size as the Brother, she came over after she'd finished, stuck out a dirty hand and asked me; "Gimme one o' them, will ya?"

Ma always told us to share and although I'd only two left, I gave her one because she scared me. Her coat was torn, and she dragged it along the ground.

When we reported back to Eddie and Da, Eddie released another of his guffaws.

"That'll be the tinker, Fagan, and the daughter. A great tinsmith and a fine musician, but they'd take the eye outta your head without you missing it."

Lots of men came looking at Eddie's bullocks and one, with a mad foxy head, began by waving his arms and yelling numbers at Eddie, who shook his head. Later,

Ginger returned, and after opening the bullocks' mouths and looking at their teeth, they started all over again, twirling arms, bawling out figures, and patting each other's backs. It looked like someone had put sticky-backs or itching powder down their shirts. Then, after an age, Eddie spat on his palm and the other man spat on his and they shook hands.

It went quiet. With my gob wide open like I was trying to catch flies, I watched as the redheaded man pulled a bundle of money the size of a turnip from his coat pocket, removed an elastic band, and counted pound after pound into Eddie's hand till he'd a pile as thick as Da's prayer book. They shook hands once more, and the man led away the bullocks.

Uncle Eddie turned, his face gleaming.

"We won't be walking home tonight, lads."

Into the pub with us. The place rammed with other farmers, some happy, others with long pusses, and it wasn't the same as any of the pubs Da took us to. The bar stood in one corner with high stools. Next to it another counter where you could buy bread and butter and cans of oil and anything else you wanted. Bicycle wheels and tyres dangled from a hook set into the ceiling. Down at the far end, in a dark section, a man with bulging eyes flaked lumps of meat with a cleaver. His once-white coat dripped with blood like Frankenstein. He seemed happy.

Da got two stools and me and the Brother hopped up.

"Two drops, two pints, and give my helpers whatever they want," Eddie said to the barman, "and put away three of your finest T-bone steaks."

Ma had said the stout must've worked and killed all my worms, and I didn't have to drink the black stuff anymore, so I had orange and the Brother lemonade. Eddie got us bucket-sized bags of toffee bonbons and slipped each of us a shiny half-crown. Buttercup and Rainbow got a treat as well. Juicy bones from the Frankenstein man.

After the Angelus at six, Eddie started singing, rattling off songs by the Everly Brothers and Buddy Holly. Everybody joined in, roaring more than singing and full of sweets, crisps and orange, my eyes tried to close.

"'Tis time to hit the road, boys," Da said. "I'll organise the hackney man, so go and do a wee before we leave."

He came back with the guy with the short leg. Eddie collected the steaks and bought a box of chocolates with a ribbon and a small bottle of sherry, and we were off.

The dogs jumped into the boot, and Da and Eddie sang all the way till I got sick. The driver cursed. Da said the effing word and lit a cigarette.

There was no Rosary said that evening, and I couldn't sleep because Da snored so much it rattled the tiny panes of glass in the window.

Next morning after he'd done his business, Da, spade in hand, took me off to dig spuds for the dinner. The hens followed.

"Don't let anyone ever tell you hens are stupid. As bright as ourselves and cuter than foxes, they are. When they see the shovel, they know there's digging to be done and where there's digging, there are worms, and the best worms are where potatoes are grown."

Da was right. They hardly waited for the ground to be turned before they started picking and poking, chuckling away like it was their Christmas Day.

The spuds got a rinse before going into the skillet pot and Da helped load the frying pan. In went the steaks and Ma piled heaps of onions and mushrooms on top. My mouth watered when the sizzling started. Ma chucked a fist of salt and a lump of butter into the pot when the potatoes burst into balls of flour.

Then she treated herself to a glass of the sherry. A small glass, not much bigger than an egg cup.

A steak each, dark as chocolate, for Da, Eddie and Ma, who cut long slivers the length of rulers off hers for me and the Brother. Rainbow and Buttercup, sprawled in front of the fire, like they owned the place, got the bones.

When we finished, I licked my plate, and nobody gave out to me. Then Ma made tea and opened the chocolates.

"No rummaging in the second layer till the top one's gone," she ordered.

"This is the best party ever, Uncle Eddie," I said. "I hope you make loads more money the next time you sell your bollocks."

Da looked at Ma. Ma looked at Da. They both looked at Eddie, who looked as if he might wet himself. It didn't matter that I didn't understand, because everyone laughed, and the Brother sneaked a toffee from the bottom tier.

Secrets

"We'll be travelling to the river tomorrow to cut rushes for the thatch," Eddie announced.

"Can I come, Da, please, please? I promise I won't get sick."

"Never mind the vomit," Ma said. "They can't stand still for five seconds. Who'll be keeping an eye when the pair of you are cutting and gathering, and what if one of them falls in?"

"Whisht. They'll be fine. Sure, the water is never more than a foot or so deep."

"I'm worried already. Not a wink of sleep will I get."

Da picked up the newspaper, and that was that.

Before bedtime, Eddie took me over to Deirdre's shed and I helped take down a basket, as big as Ma's water barrel, from the rafters.

"I never even saw that before. What's it for?"

"We'll use it to carry all our bits 'n' pieces and bring home the rushes. 'Tis made of rushes itself. Almost waterproof. See for yourself."

I tried to look inside, but even standing on my tippy-toes, could barely peep over the top.

In the morning, we'd to wait for the bread to cool before heading off. Ma packed the basket. I could smell the brown loaf, wrapped in two tea cloths, together with the treat of a pack of sausages.

"Keep the grub away from the paraffin or you'll be eating nothing, and don't take your eyes off the pair of them."

Me and the Brother wore our wellies, Da and Eddie brought along funny looking boots.

"They're called waders," Da said.

We emptied the basket on the riverbank. Out came

Eddie's tools, a primus to boil water, a frying pan the size of a saucer to cook the sausages, and bottles too – one full of water, one with milk and four bottles of stout that Eddie snuck in when Ma wasn't looking.

Da put on the waders. He looked as funny as a circus clown, with the baggy yokes almost reaching his neck.

"We'll make a camp with the basket, Da."

"Do what ye want with it. Just stay away from the edge."

First, we watched as Eddie went into the water with a slasher knife and cut two yokes with furry bits at the top.

"They're bulrushes," he told us.

Eddie poured a tiny drop of paraffin on the tips and lit them. With a satisfying *whoosh*, they lit up. Flaming torches. One for the Brother and one for me.

"This is the best fun ever," the Brother said. "I think I'll be Geronimo, or maybe pretend they're flamethrowers."

We ran and explored till the flames burnt out, dashed back to camp and Eddie made two more and off we galloped, Rainbow and Buttercup alongside, but they didn't enjoy the flaming bulrushes too much.

Da and Eddie cut about a million rushes and lay them on the riverbank to dry where we'd set up camp, and when our bellies began rumbling, Eddie began cooking.

Minutes after getting the primus going with the paraffin, the pan sitting on top started hissing like a swarm of bees, and he threw on the sausages. They cooked in minutes. Some got burnt, but it didn't matter. Da made sandwiches, and the four of us sat underneath a tree heavy with crow's nests, on old raincoats Ma made us take.

"Ye never know, it could lash before the dinner."

We gobbled everything before the wasps attacked, and Da pulled two Crunchie bars out of his pockets, one for me and one for the Brother. And with the sun roasting, me, the

Brother and uncle Eddie, who looked like a bald gorilla with his hairy belly, took off our shirts. Da glanced over at Eddie and rolled up his shirt sleeves.

We left them sitting with their backs against the tree having a smoke and a bottle of porter and headed off exploring. The basket caught the Brother's eye again.

"I've an idea. Let's put it in the water and see if it floats."

Anytime the Brother came up with an idea, there was never a happy ending.

"Can't do that," I said, standing there with arms folded. "Da will kill us."

"Coward."

In went the basket and in he went, rocking the basket from side to side.

"Look at this. Let's pretend it's a battleship or even a flying saucer. Come on, you scaredy cat."

What else could I do? He was the Big Brother, so I hopped in and hung on as it wobbled, but only a few drops got in.

With rushes and reeds surrounding us, we didn't get far, so the Brother gave it a yank. Then it moved. Off towards the middle of the river we headed. Going around a corner, the channel widened, flowed faster - as did the basket. I got scared and wanted out.

"I need a wee."

"Shut up and hold on. This is brilliant."

With the water now seeping through to the top of my wellies, I lifted the leg of my khaki shorts and did a sneaky widdle down the side.

"Hold on, Son! Dear Jesus, hold on, Son!"

I looked and saw Da, arms waving, going mental, running along the riverbank, Eddie trying his best to keep up.

"Hiya, Da!" the Brother shouted.

"Don't panic, lads. Don't panic. I'll save ye," Eddie said, sploshing about, his shiny head bobbing up and down like a lost football before letting out a roar. "I can't swim!"

Da, down to his underpants, dived in. I didn't even know *he* could swim. As he grabbed the basket, it lurched to one side. We hung on. I screamed. My Da didn't have boxers' muscles, but dragged the wickerwork against the current and hauled it – and the floundering Eddie, who spewed a mixture of river water and porter every time his noggin appeared – to the riverside.

Silence.

Horses pant, puff, and snort after a race. We did the same.

Da's face was the colour of ice-cream, and he didn't look well or happy.

"Dear Jesus, what did I tell you? What did I tell you? Keep away from the river? What did I tell you?"

More silence.

I thought we'd get a right walloping, but he grabbed and hugged us so tightly it almost hurt. Eddie collected sticks from the base of the tree, lit a fire and made tarry sugary tea. I'm sure the crows had a great time gaping at us, huddled around in our underpants, trying to dry our clothes.

"Now, listen boys," Da started. "Sometimes, us men must have secrets, just between men, real men. Do you understand?"

We nodded.

"Well, lads, I think what happened today should be a secret. Our secret. We won't tell Ma what took place, and if you promise to keep the secret, I'll give each of you a half-crown."

A simple decision. We nodded like a pair of old men. Real men.

Night hadn't yet come when we started the trek home, but the hedgerows threw long shadows and most of the birds were asleep. Da and Eddie carried the basket, overflowing with rushes.

"They take months to dry," Eddie told us. "It'll be next Summer before I show ye how to thatch."

"What was that?" the Brother asked on hearing a scraping noise coming from the ditch ahead. I took a step closer to Da and held his hand.

"Yera, 'tis nothing," said Eddie. "Probably a badger of a fox out trying to catch his dinner, although it might well be the pùca."

"The wha-?" asked the Brother.

"The pùca. Surely, you've heard of him. A bad bit 'o stuff he is. You'd want to have no truck with him. They say he goes searching for young boys at night."

"Jeez, Eddie, will you shut up? Haven't we had enough excitement for one day?"

"I'll tell ye all about the fairies and the pùca some other time so."

I'm glad he forgot.

"Now, to change the subject, did you ever think of marrying?"

"Yera, there were plenty lassies got a crossbar home from a céilí, but sure didn't most of them take off for the bright lights of London and Dublin as soon as they'd a few shillings put aside. The ones left behind either had a bit of a want or had to look after elderly parents after the rest of the flock fled the nest."

"That's kind of sad."

"Maybe 'tis. Molly Flaherty got notions about me at one stage, and we walked out for a time. When she'd the war paint and a rub of lipstick and a flowery dress on, she wasn't too bad on the eye."

"What happened?"

"What happened? I'll tell you what happened. One dreary afternoon, when a heavy sky and mist hid the grass itself, I took a notion and wandered over the hills to her place, arriving as she closed the four-bar gate after milking the pair of cows. She smiled, and I watched as she wiped hands, the colour of the earth, down the front of her geansaí. That jumper, I'd say, belonged to her father, or maybe her grandfather. I won't be unkind, but that evening, she'd a head on her that looked like a furze bush after a lightning strike, and that brought the romance to a finish. So, nothing sad about it. If you saw the state of Molly now, you'd say it was the luckiest day of my life."

Eddie's guffaw scared Buttercup and Rainbow, loyally walking beside him like shadows.

We were home.

Arms folded, Ma waited.

"Jesus, what kept ye? You had me worried sick. I expected ye back hours ago."

"Would you stop worrying, woman?" We'd a mighty day, didn't we, lads?"

"The best day ever, Ma," we replied in perfect harmony.

August slipped away, and the time came to head home, to school, work, and the daily scrubbing of shirt collars.

I wanted to stay forever.

Cases packed, Da wore a tie for the first time since we left Dublin, and Ma wore her flowery dress, all set for the long haul.

"Come on," said Ma, "we'll collect a few eggs. I'll carry them back home in my handbag."

She'd four in her hands when her high heels slipped in the chicken shit and she almost fell, but one egg broke and slithered down the front of her dress.

And Ma said the terrible bad word.

"I'm telling Da what you said."

"Don't you dare… I'll tell you what we'll do instead. It'll be our secret. Just between you and me, and when we get home, I'll buy you a big box of Smarties in McCarthy's."

"Only Smarties, Ma? Da gives us a half-crown to keep his secrets."

Part 3

The Kingdom

The Kingdom

"We're here," Da proclaimed, standing in the carriage, arms outstretched. Da was a great man for stretching out the arms when making a point, but he got a right wallop on the noggin when the train hit the buffers and he went flying. Ma giggled, and that didn't go down too well with Da.

"We're back in county Kerry, the Kingdom," he continued, like he did every time we came to spend our holliers in Killarney with his da, Jack.

"There are only two Kingdoms. The Kingdom of God and the Kingdom of Kerry." Then he lit a fag and took down our cases.

Ma yawned. It wasn't like going to Uncle Eddie's, but the train took all day, stopping at hundreds of stations, and Ma said I was always as cranky as a weasel by the time we arrived.

Jack stood on the platform. His pipe, almost as big as himself, sent puffs of smoke into the sky like Geronimo and the other Indians used to do. Me and the Brother never called him Grandad or Grandpa. We called him Jack like everyone did. Everyone in Killarney knew him.

"I don't know where they got you," Ma said to Da. "You're as tall as a telegraph pole and look at Jack, not the size of a jockey."

Jack's house, a hen's kick from the station, meant Da didn't have to go looking for a taxi man. Jack wore a hat, Da called it a fedora, and never took it off. Not in the house or the toilet or anywhere, unless when saying his prayers.

We didn't have to do our business outside, because Jack had a toilet in a shed out the back. The shed had more holes in the rusty roof than Deirdre's shed up in Uncle Eddie's place. The bockety seat, made from bits of wood from an orange box, was always wet. Da said something called condensation caused it, but sometimes if I couldn't climb up, and if I only wanted to do a wee, I'd stand on the floor and aim… and miss most of the time. But it didn't matter, because it was only a muck floor, anyway. And Da must have learned how to make toilet paper from his Da because Jack had some hanging from a nail in the shed. He made his from *The Kerryman* newspaper.

The house had two rooms downstairs with concrete floors blacker than soot. Jack slept in one and Ma did all the washing, cooking and all the other stuff in the other room and she was lucky because Jack had a gas ring in the corner, and she didn't have to cook on the open fire.

Jack never closed his front door, because people were "always dropping in for the chat", and at night his best friends, about six or seven of them, came to play cards. Most limped along with sticks, but a few cycled on old rickety bikes, and Ma said, "I don't know if it's auld bones or the bikes that're creaking the most." All of them smoked pipes. Ma said she could never figure out how they played the game.

"Sure, isn't the deck of cards as black as the grate in the fire and as sticky as tar? 'Tis all that blowing and scraping and farting with them pipes. Yuck."

The old men played for a penny, or threepence on pension day. Me and the Brother didn't know how to play, but watched.

Everyone got five cards and held them close so no one could peep. They took turns dealing, and when that job was done, they lay the rest of the deck in the middle of the table, with the top one turned up so everyone could see it. Then the racket started. They'd put their cards down one by one until some auld fella let out a roar– "Beat that!" – as he hit the table a flake with the side of his fist after playing the winner… or so he thought.

"Indeed'n I will," some other auld codger would cry as a better card hit the table with a louder thump. Ma had to take the milk bottle off the table every night because it would have been smashed, as the table jumped up and down like it was doing an Irish jig.

Games went on till late, but Ma only let us watch for a while, because the smoke was like thick fog.

"Your clothes will stink, and I'm getting a headache from it. C'mon, time for bed."

Upstairs had two rooms. One for Ma and Da, me and the Brother in the other where we slept in an ancient iron and brass bed. As soon as anybody put a foot on the stairs it wobbled and squeaked, and we'd to take giant steps, because some of the wood was broken, and you'd fall through if you weren't careful. Da tried loads of times to fix them with wood from an orange box, but Ma said he'd only made them worse.

"And never try to open them windows," Da ordered with a wag of his cigarette-stained middle finger.

"The cord is rotten in them, and they'd take off your fingers like a guillotine. If necessary, *I'll* open them." When opened, he'd jam a stick under it. Da was a great man with the orange boxes.

Four brass knobs and brass rails decorated our rickety iron bed. Ma always gave it a polishing, and when she did, it shone like Uncle Eddie's head.

Da thought the old relic might be valuable. "Might be worth a few bob someday."

"Don't be fooling yourself," Ma told him. "The brass is fine, but sure, it's only rust that's holding the rest of it together."

The Brother discovered he could screw off the brass knobs, and they were hollow.

"If we were spies, t'would be a great place to hide secrets. I'll think of something." An' his eyes did that thing like the baddies in pictures, when they're plottin' bank robberies.

100

Murder in the Air

In Uncle Eddie's, the stupid rooster woke us every morning with his cock-a-doodle-doos. Down in Jack's, it was horses neighing quietly and scraping their hooves. That's how they called for their breakfast. Black ones, brown ones, big and small, dozens lived in a stable next to our house.

Da said people, thousands, came on holidays from all over the world to see the Lakes of Killarney, and as they'd no cars, they'd go on posh horse and carts.

"They're called jaunting cars," he told us. "With a jarvey in charge of each." The man who owned the stables and horses lived in our lane as well, and every night, he'd brush the horses' hair and wash the jaunting cars. After putting the horses to bed, he would polish the leather straps and brass buckles. When he finished, he would pull the jaunting cars all by himself and line them in a row, like chariots, ready for the next day. And I'd sit on the footpath watching, hoping he'd ask me to help because I loved the smells of the horses and the leather.

And if the horses didn't wake us, it was the walloping and flaking of steel coming from the forge another bit down the lane. A forge is like a cobbler's, but for horses. Da took us to watch Mr Sullivan work over a roasting fire pit, sweat pouring like a river down his forehead, and he looked like a black man but wasn't, and over a string vest he wore a long leather apron that came down to his ankles. It had a pouch in the front with loads of funny-looking tools and knives and with muscles in his arms like Desperate Dan's. He kind of scared me.

"Watch the way Padraig makes the shoes. First, he'll measure the horse's hoof, like the lady does when you get new shoes in Clarke's. Then the hoof gets a trim. It's like when we cut our toenails. In the fire pit, he'll get the coal as hot as Hell using that bellows, and when the steel goes white, he'll beat the shite out of it on that thing over there, it's called an anvil, till it goes into the right shape and to finish, he'll make the holes for the nails."

"This is Billy," Mr Sullivan told us. "The oldest and gentlest fella I've ever put shoes on. If it's OK with your Da, the pair of ye can help as long as ye don't stand behind him. You can never tell. We don't want to be going to a funeral."

We were in the door before Da could open his gob.

The Brother got the job of firing up the pit with the bellows, and we could hear the air whish into the belly of the fire when he opened and closed the yoke. The first shoe didn't fit right, so Padraig did the job again. He heated, flaked, and dipped the red-hot shoe into a barrel of water, sending a cloud of smelly steam up through the roof, before holding it with a long tong to Billy's hoof. The hoof burned and filled the place with a horrible smell like rotten eggs. The place looked and smelt like a torture chamber, or maybe even a witch's place. It was brilliant.

"He's fine." Padraig told us. "They don't feel a thing. Now, that's it. Hand me them nails. Six of 'em."

He said that to me. I felt about as big as Da and could see the Brother had a puss on him.

"Gimme them one by one."

And, as he held Billy's hoof held between his knees, I handed over the nails as if they were grenades. In they went and to finish, Padraig used a long file thing to take off any bit of nail that stuck out.

Job done, the man who'd sat outside on a wobbly chair, reading the racing pages and smoking fags, led Billy away.

As I'd crossed soldier off my list of things to do when I grew up, I'd add blacksmith to the list when we got home after our holidays.

Between the station and our lane stood the swankiest hotel in town, the Great Southern. A massive place like a castle with ivy growing up the walls and a red carpet on steps to welcome guests to a revolving door. A man as tall as Da, dressed in a fancy coat and top hat said "Hello" to all the rich people as they arrived and said "Goodbye" to all the local gougers as soon as they put a foot on the bottom step.

Like a forest, thousands of trees, bigger than *Jack and the Beanstalk* ones, surrounded the hotel and our lane. Hundreds of millions of crows lived in them, and when they flew off in the morning and came back at teatime to go to sleep, the sky turned as black as Da's shoe polish.

Ma warned us, "Keep your hands on your heads and don't be gawking up at them. I've enough to be doing without washing bird shite from your heads."

When the jarveys came to get the horses ready, the Brother helped, because he was nine and three-quarters, and once the horses had their reins on and were tied to the jaunting cars, they'd head off, clippity-clop, clippity-clop, like in a procession, heading to the hotel or the railway station to collect the people, and the horses started doing their business, because they were after eating straw and hay. That's what horses have for breakfast. They don't like porridge. And we didn't mind all the horse shite in our lane and outside Jack's house, because the smell was kind of nice, and even if you stood in some, it didn't stick to your shoe like dog shit, and anyway it didn't matter because the floor in Jack's house was cement, and black.

And sometimes, the man with the horses let the Brother sit up with him and hold the reins, and I'd be left standing there. And when they passed, he'd look down, laugh, and stick out his tongue, and that made me sad, and mad, and I'd plan to chop off his head with the bread knife when he came back.

103

The Nerves

Da said that smoking was good for the nerves, and because we shattered his, he smoked a lot. Jack preferred a pipe, and after our porridge, we'd watch him get ready for his first smoke of the day. He'd start by scraping out all the old tobacco stuff with a penknife as old and worn out as himself. Then he'd blow and suck on the bit that went in his mouth and sometimes he'd spit into the fireplace and my porridge would do somersaults in my belly. After cutting off tiny slices from a block of tobacco, he'd rub them together and pack them in the pipe. Job done, he'd sit back, strike a match, take a deep pull, and disappear in a cloud. He even had a silver lid with holes in it. He'd fill the house with smoke, and I loved the smell – much nicer than the smell from Da's fags.

Around that time, the Brother started puffing.

"I need it for me nerves," he told me as we ran around the streets playing cops 'n' robbers.

"Maybe I might give you a pull," he said. I wasn't too sure; My nerves were OK, I thought. I was seven and three-quarters.

"I've been collecting," he said, opening a matchbox. It was full of butts. "They're all Da's, and when they go for their walk, I'm going to make a fag."

"How?"

"Simple. We'll break up these little ones and cut a bit of newspaper the same size as a ciggie and put in the tobacco and roll it up tight, like a real cigarette. One lad at school does it all the time. His nerves are in bits, and if he hasn't enough tobacco, he mixes in some tea leaves."

We'd no car, so Ma and Da went for walks and we'd be dragged along. All the way down by the lakes or out as far as Ross Castle. It was miles away.

It wasn't too bad when we got there because we'd skim stones across the water. Da was a brilliant skimmer. Once a stone did ten jumps before it sank. One of mine did five. Rowing boats belonging to fishermen were tied up at the side of the lake, and me and the Brother messed around in them, rocking about as if we were pirates out at sea. All great gas, but the walking was boring... boooooring. We'd be fighting or acting the eejit most of the time and Da used to get mad, and Ma said it didn't do her any good to get out.

"If we leave you behind today, will you promise you'll behave and won't be getting into more trouble?"

"Yes, Ma," we said, like a pair of parrots.

And off they went. The Brother got scissors and got started. His fag looked funny. It was a lot longer and fatter than Da's. Maybe the Brother's nerves *were* terrible after all.

"We'll smoke it upstairs," he said. "I'll open the window so the smoke can escape."

I wasn't too sure about all this "We'll do this" and "We'll do that" business, but what could I do?

The Brother got the window open without losing his hand and lit up. He'd a few flames to begin with, but after they went out, he took a few puffs, sitting on the edge of the bed, legs crossed, like an auld fella. When he turned pale, he gave it to me.

"Here, you can have one or two pulls."

I sucked in, and when the burning hit my belly, I started coughing and spluttering, and my eyes went watery.

"Are you up there?"

"Janey, they're back. Shhh. They shouldn't be back yet."

"Are you up there?"

I heard the stairs creaking, and my watery eyes turned to tears.

The Brother leapt into action. He screwed off one of the

brass knobs, dropped the cigarette in, and put the knob back.

"What are you doing?"

"Nothing."

"Hmm, nothing, is it?"

"We were tired after playing," the Brother said, and even I knew it was a stupid answer.

"And who opened the window?"

"I did, because we were sweating, weren't we?"

I wasn't before, but after he'd brought me into the crime, my vest clung to my back.

Da turned to go when he saw something. "Jeez, where's that smoke coming from?"

Smoke signals rose from the bedpost. We stood glued to the floor as Da took the stairs in two giant steps, grabbed the teapot, bounded back up and soaked everything with lukewarm tea.

"You could've burnt the house down, so you could," he said, dragging each of us by an ear down the stairs. Ma missed the action because she was doing her business in the shed. That's why they'd come back early, but Da gave her the details and lit a fag.

"Asking the pair of you not to get into trouble is like asking that fire not to burn," Ma said, and I think she tried to be cross, but I saw her smile as well, and because we were on our holliers, we didn't get the wooden spoon. Or maybe Jack didn't have one.

Da went out for a few pints.

Part 4

The Real Capital

The Move

Back home, back to school, back to homework. I hated it.

"They've confirmed my promotion, Dear."

Da had come home late. His face looked like he'd been standing in front of a fire, but I think he'd been sitting in a pub. As happy as a dog with nine tails, and all nine wagging. Ma started crying.

"What's promotion, Da?" the Brother asked.

"Promotion is like being in the army, Son. You've seen it in the pictures. The private becomes a sergeant, then a captain and..."

"And then a general, Da."

"Well, yes, eventually. There's promotion in my job as well. Every time I get promoted; I get more money at the end of the month."

"Ma says there's never enough at the end of the month, don't you, Ma?"

"Well, yes, sometimes we run short," Da said before Ma could get in, but anyway, she was all sobs and sighs.

"Whenever I get the promotion, I have to go to a different office, and that's why we've to move again."

"Are you a general in your job, Da?"

"Not quite, Son. Clerical Grade 5, to be exact."

"Ma says we're like Travellers."

Da lit a fag.

Our house had been sad since Da came home months earlier, all excited, telling us about his chance of getting a new job and us moving to Cork.

"What about all my friends? Do I have to start all over again? When we moved and bought this house, you said, 'That's it. No more moves.' "

Ma dabbed her eyes with the corner of a hankie with flowers on it and then blew snots from her nose.

"And what about Mango?" the Brother asked.

Da gave a gigantic sigh. "Miss Daly said she'll look after Mango."

"She hates cats, Da."

Then my new baby brother joined in with Ma and started wailing. Because of him, we couldn't go back to Uncle Eddie's and do the thatching that Summer. Ma had a massive belly and could barely do the shopping and the cooking and the washing and the ironing and the scrubbing of Da's collars without getting tired.

After the baby popped out of her belly, Da took me and the Brother to see her the next day.

"Da took us to the pub last night, Ma, when it was dark," I blurted.

"Could you not have given it a miss for the one night?"

"Had to wet the child's head, Dear," said Da, but I think he was cross with me. Maybe going to the pub was another one of our secrets, but he said nothing about a half-crown.

Our new brother was tiny. He couldn't do anything, only cry and do his gick, and Ma had to wash and scrub thousands of nappies. The clothesline was full of them, all different whites. Sometimes, if he did a real messy one, Ma would hold the nappy in the toilet and give it a flush to get rid of some shite, but once or twice, the nappy escaped and disappeared down the loo. Ma made us promise not to tell Da and gave us Crunchie bars.

When our lav started overflowing, Da got cross, and he'd have to borrow rods from Kev's da, and he'd be out on the road, pushing loads of the rod things through miles of pipes and tons of shite.

"Are the pipes blocked?" a neighbour asked as he passed by.

"Nah, I'm just doing this for a bit of relaxation," Da

said, but he used the effer word as well, and the man never spoke to Da again.

Whoosh… the water, and everything else, went gushing when Da got the pipes working and he stood there real proud, like a fisherman after catching a fish, with a dirty nappy hanging, dripping, from the end of a rod.

"I wonder how that got there?" he'd say to Ma, and she'd say nothing.

Sometimes, I think Ma enjoyed talking about being like Travellers.

"First a flat in Sligo, Grade 2, then on to Galway, Grade 3. That's when you came along, and we lived in a flat over a shop. I'll never forget that Christmas Day till the day I die."

"Was I bold, Ma?"

"No, no, no, you weren't. Sure, weren't you only a couple of months old, but *that* little devil was bold, broke my heart so you did," she said, wagging a finger at the Brother.

"Ah, Ma, you're always telling people that story, and I can feel me face getting all red when you tell them."

Ignoring him, she told her tale again.

"There I was on Christmas morning, doing my best to make it a nice day for you all, a borrowed tablecloth from Mrs Maughan on the table, all her fancy plates, big and small ones, and them all matching, Wedgewood they were, neatly laid out on the cloth."

"You forgot about the bowls for the Christmas pudding, Ma," I added.

"Shut up, you, you eejit," snapped the Brother.

"It was only a tiny turkey, not much bigger than a chicken… Da got a bargain just before the butcher's closed, but when I'd it settled in the oven, the smell was like heaven, and I'd put a ring of spuds all around the turkey

110

and they roasted away, going a golden brown, and the smell from the gravy I'd made with the turkey giblets made my mouth water, and the Brussel sprouts were minding their own business, boiling away, and then – and then—"

"Ah, Ma, you've told us what happened thousands of times," the Brother begged.

"And I'll tell it another thousand times. No wonder me hair is the colour of a badger. Now, where was I? Yes, Da was doing the crossword and said he thought a nappy needed changing, and after turning down the saucepans, I told you, you little blighter, not to touch anything. I wasn't gone from the kitchen for five seconds – not five seconds! – when I heard the crash. I still don't know how a four-year-old could've pulled that tablecloth and everything, every... single... thing, onto the floor. Thank the Good Lord that the gravy and all the other roasting hot stuff weren't on the table, or you'd have been scalded to death."

"Ah, Ma, don't be telling everyone."

"I will so. You were only four back then and wouldn't do what you were told, and now you're ten, and you're still acting the eejit. I'll never forget it. Eating our dinner off cracked plates on Christmas Day."

"Then, after only a year – Dublin, Grade 4, and now onto Cork, Grade 5. Travellers, I'm telling you, we're like Travellers."

Da said we mightn't be living in Cork for long because he might get promoted again.

"It'll probably be back to Dublin when it happens, so not much point in buying a house at this stage."

"Will you be a general then, Da?"

"Not quite, Son, but getting closer."

He travelled down to find a place to rent, and Ma packed our stuff and put it in tea chests. A man with a lorry came and gave us stacks of them. Da said that farmers way off out in Africa, and India, and China grew tea instead of grass, and sent it to us in those tea chests. And then the man in the Lyons Tea factory put the tea into little packets and made a fortune.

Even the Brother cried the day we left. Ma hadn't stopped for days, and Da smoked thousands of fags. A lorry, bigger than a double-decker bus, came early that Saturday and two men with big bellies and cigarettes stuck to their lips put everything Ma and Da owned into the back, filling only a teensy bit of the truck.

"Jeez, mister, is that all you've got?"

"That's the lot," said Da, handing over ten shillings. "Have a few pints when you get there."

All the neighbours were out, saying goodbyes and gawking at what we had and hadn't got.

A taxi-man came, not the one with the short leg, to take us to the station. Miss Daly and Kev's ma joined Ma, and they were all bawling. We couldn't find Mango to say goodbye, but I think he must've been sad, and went to play with his mates.

I got sad when I had to say goodbye to Kev because we were best friends and blood brothers. Once, way before Kev crashed into the bus, we both hit the kerb and went flying and cut our knees and blood gushed everywhere, and I got Kev to hold his knee right next to mine.

"It's all mixing," I told him, "like in the pictures. We'll be blood brothers, like Buffalo Bill and Sitting Bull."

Ma washed my cuts and put plasters on them, but when I told her about blood brothers, she took off the bandage, put iodine stuff on my knees and it stung like a bee sting, and my knees went the colour of oranges.

"I'm not so sure about them next door," she'd said. "Did you see the colour of her hair this week? Pink! It'd cut the eye outta you, so it would!"

112

When the time came to get into the taxi, Kev gave me a Trigger bar and a bag of bull's eye sweets and started bawling.

Ma sobbed and sighed all the way. Me and the Brother had our heads out the windows. We knew all the stations from the times we went to stay in Jack's.

Almost There

When our train stopped at T-h-u-r-l-e-s – I spelled out all the letters – Ma knitted away. It helped her stop crying, but she leapt from her seat when my glasses fell out the window. Da jumped onto the platform.

"Dear Jesus, Son, can't you be more careful?" he cried, as the man waved his green flag, and the train moved, and Da started running, and we laughed... even Ma.

"It's no laughing matter," he said after flinging himself into our compartment as the train picked up speed. "They could've left me behind."

Ma said nothing. She didn't have to.

After lots more stops, Da said, "Almost there," when the train reached a tunnel.

"It's almost a mile long, so take in your heads or you'll get covered in soot and be like kids from Africa when we arrive."

Ma carried the baby brother. Da hauled our cases, and went for a taxi, ordering me and the Brother to hold hands. We hated that. A line of taxis snaked all the way around the station, with lots of men with enormous bellies and bigger bums leaning against their chariots, talking and smoking fags.

It only took four or five or six minutes to get to our new house. I could almost count to a hundred and read the clock.

"This is it," Da said.

"It's got an upstairs," me and the Brother squealed. "It's got an upstairs, Ma, and look, look, there's a shop right next door, and another weensy one across the road."

Ma tried to be good and not cry anymore, but after going inside and down the hall, she started again.

"Is this the best you could do?" she wailed. "Good Lord, look at the place, and that colour. It's everywhere!"

114

"It's the best we can afford, Dear."

"That colour navy, dark navy, everywhere. Jeez, it's even on the ceilings, as if I wasn't depressed enough as it is. It'll be like living in a mental institution."

Me and the Brother went exploring upstairs.

"We can jump out of these windows," he said, yanking one open. "We'll make parachutes and jump."

I had a gawk around the other rooms before reporting back to Ma.

"It's the same upstairs. The bathroom is nearly black as well, and so is the ceiling."

Da gave me the look and lit a fag.

Outside, we made more discoveries. We'd a massive garden the size of a football pitch, with long grass, and trees with crows' nests.

"That's a chestnut tree," the Brother said and ran to see if he could climb it. He was an even better climber than Kev. He'd be like a gorilla, swinging from branch to branch, singing the Tarzan song Kev used to sing. Ma said it was bold, but always laughed when she heard it.

After the men with the tea chests left, Ma started putting stuff away. We wanted Da to cut the grass so we could play football, but we'd no mower and anyway, Ma had things for him to do first. She didn't have to shout or anything. She just said, "Get paint and get rid of that colour."

Da lit another cigarette.

The lady next door called to say hello and said she'd a little girl the same age as me. Ma saw her heading off to school the next day.

"Ah, would you look at the little pet? She's like something you'd dangle from a key ring. Isn't she sweet, trotting off like that, and her hair in pigtails? And that red plaid pinafore is just gorgeous. Wouldn't it be lovely to have a quiet little girl around about the house, instead of what I have, two brats, and the small fella crawling around who'll no doubt follow suit?"

"Janey Mac, Ma, are you going to get fat again and have another one?" the Brother asked, all concerned.

"Lord, no. I'm only joking. I'll stick with the three of ye, bad an' all as you are." Then she looked in the lopsided mirror Da had hung from a nail in the kitchen, seeing if anymore "grey invaders" had arrived.

Because the Brother was going to be eleven, he went to a school in town. All the teachers were Christian Brothers like our school in Dublin, but these must have been special Brothers because Da had to pay piles of money to them, and Ma had to buy him a special blazer and get him long trousers – his first pair.

"You look very smart in that uniform, a proper gent. I only hope you behave like one," Ma said.

And we had to have chips every day till the end of that month, and it wasn't even January.

I wished I could've got longers as well, because on wintry days, my short hairy trousers rubbed against my knees and they got red and sore, like you'd rubbed them with sandpaper, and I'd to walk slowly like that time I'd done a load because of the marble-playing bollocks. Ma said they were chaffed, and put cream on to take away the pain, but the same thing happened every day till the Summer came.

"Are they all nice boys?" she asked after my first day at the primary school down the road.

"I don't know. They started laughing when the teacher made me stand up and say my name."

"Oh, I wonder why they did that, but don't worry, I'm sure you'll make loads of new friends."

And one day after school, when I kicked my football into the garden next door, Ma said I could get it, but not to jump over the wall.

116

"Use the gate," she said, "and be polite if anyone says anything."

I ran and got the ball, and the girl came from nowhere and asked me my name and when I told her, she told me hers.

"I'm six an' a quarter," she said. "Do you want to see my knickers?"

I was polite, like Ma told me. "Thank you," I said, and she lifted her pinafore and showed me. They were yellow. I ran home and told Ma, who peeped out through the net curtains and saw the girl playing with her dolls.

"Maybe 'tis better to have all boys after all," she muttered.

Survival

My new school had only two classrooms and must have been thousands of years old. The windows rattled anytime a lorry passed, and it had a fireplace like the one in Uncle Eddie's, with a cage all around it, like in the zoo, to stop anyone falling into the flames.

I tried to do good ABC's in my writing, but the desk they gave me wobbled, and my dipping pen skeeted across the page, and my hands got covered in ink. The teachers press, stuffed with stuff, leaned to one side and whenever the master banged the doors, one of them swung open, and after he'd banged it a few times, all the panes of glass rattled, but not the ones that were missing, and he'd put a bit of cardboard between the doors and shut it that way, and I heard him whisper a curse because I sat next to it.

"Do you know, I'm thinking you've got the worms back. I'll get you a dose from the chemist one of these days." Ma used to tell me, so I must have been as skinny as a rasher, and had roundy dispensary glasses, and a Dublin accent. A *Crumlin* accent. And I didn't understand some things they were talking about in my new school. Like they called their schoolbags "sacks", and runners were called "rubber dollies", and some said Cork was the Real Capital of Ireland.

They're all mad down here, I thought, and when you've things like that flying around in your head, there could be trouble on the way.

I tried to be brave, but after a week, I knew I had to do two things. Run as fast as lightning, and lose the accent. I had to because Chimp told me, "I'm going to thump you after school."

Chimp wasn't his real name, but he looked and walked like a gorilla, and sat in a desk all on his own at the back of the classroom. Yep, I needed to steer clear of Chimp. And the teacher, lots older, but not as tall as Da, had a shiny head and a purple nose, and his shirt always had huge yellow stains under his arms, and he smelt like a dirty dishcloth.

He didn't have a leather belt to wallop us, like the Christian Brothers had. He'd a long bamboo that went *whiiiish*. I didn't want to get lashed with that. The man terrified me.

He barked at me one day when I didn't bring any sticks for the fire, but nobody told me we'd to bring some to keep the massive fire going, so he could stand in front of it all day long burning his arse.

Da said he'd bring me to school the next day "And sort your man out". But Ma wouldn't let him.

After the thing with the firewood, I didn't want to get into any more trouble with Mr Lightbulb. That wasn't the teacher's proper name, but everyone called him Lightbulb because his face turned bright red when he got cross – and he was cross most of the time.

"For your homework, I want you to use your imaginations, if you can find them." His hands waving all round like a madman. "Express yourselves, expand your vocabulary, think like Beckett and Joyce or even Dickens and Shakespeare."

I hadn't a clue who or what he was talking about but watched him getting all worked up. There was white stuff all round the corner of his mouth, and it glued me to my seat.

"Over the weekend, write a story. We'll call it a composition. Nice writing. No spidery scrawls please, one page of your copybook." Then he shut up.

"What'll we write about, sir?"

"That's where your imagination comes in."

He looked around, farted, and pointed at the cluttered cupboard.

119

"Alright, tell me all about this cupboard." Then he went outside for a fag, coughed from his toenails, snorted like a pig, and spat. The porridge in my belly did a head-over-heels.

"Ma, I've to write a composit... compostit... I've to write a story for homework."

"That's nice. What do you have to write about?"

"The stupid press in the classroom. What'll I write about that?"

"You'll think of something."

And I did. And I used my imagination, like the great Lightbulb told us to, and on Monday morning, one by one, we'd to stand by the fire and read our stories. My hands were shaking and sticky when I started.

"In the press, there are loads of things. There are lots of copybooks and there are two boxes of chalk. One is white chalk, and the other is all colours. Red, and blue, and yellow. There are pictures of Holy God, and biscuit tins, and you could find anything you want in the cupboard. Everything from a tin of paint to a bottle of whiskey—"

He stopped me as I was building up a bit of speed, and his face didn't go red. It went *purple* to match his nose.

"What did you say, boy? Read that again."

He grabbed the cane, and *whiiished* it, and I felt a wee coming.

"Read it, boy, read that last sentence."

"Everything from a tin of paint to a bottle of whiskey, sir."

It was the only time I got the cane. I didn't go to school the next day. Da went instead and "Sorted your man".

The yard looked like a minefield in the war pictures, all holes and rocks, and no grass. It didn't matter. Everyone played football. About twenty-six or even twenty-nine on each team, and because I'd learned to run fast, I scored lots of goals, and my glasses got smashed every week, and the man in the shop who used to fix them said to Da, "If you put them on the bus, they'd find their own way here," and he laughed, but Da didn't because it cost ten bob. Da put plasters and sticky tape on them sometimes, but that did no good and I stopped wearing them when playing.

The ball always went over the wall into the ditches behind, and Chimp's job was to get it. He didn't play ball. One day the ball flew in real far, right into the brambles. Chimp had to use a stick because the nettles were taller than him, and he didn't want to get stung, and when he tripped over something, he said a million curse words.

"There's the flipping ball," he said. "I tripped over a bottle. There're hundreds of them, all small whiskey bottles. I wonder how they got there?"

I used my imagination.

In the Book

The shop next door sold everything, and Ma said it was handy, and she made new friends because she went in and out about a hundred times a day. Sometimes, if the small brother started whinging, she'd give me or the Brother a list and a few shillings, and we'd give the list to the man, and he'd give us the groceries.

When Ma got to know him a bit better, and when she'd no money in her purse, the man had a copybook in a drawer with all the money and wrote what she'd bought. And sometimes she'd tell us, "Tell him to put it in the book." Ma said it was called "buying on tick", and when Da gave her money at the end of the month, the man added up all the ticks, and Ma paid him.

"I'll go to the shop for you, Ma, if you like," I heard the Brother say.

I heard Ma whispering to Da. "I don't know what's after coming over him. Maybe 'tis the posh school, but he's trying to be nice. I can't get over it."

Da gave us sixpence for our pocket money every Sunday, and we'd dart to the little shop across the road. The man was the size of a baby elephant, and he only opened the shop when he felt like it, and he sold fags and sweets, sweets that'd last, like toffee bars and aniseed balls and gobstoppers. My money and sweets were always gone before Tuesday, but sometimes, the Brother had some left on Friday or even Saturday, and he'd be sticking his tongue out and be slurping away on a Blackjack or something.

And when Ma called in to "fix up", it was the lady, the one Ma said had a head like a flowerpot, who got out the copybook. And instead of adding up all the ticks, she wrote a long list of all the bits bought on "tick". The man who owned the shop never used to do that.

When she came back, Ma banged the front door so hard the glass rattled it got such a fright, and then I heard her rummaging in the kitchen drawer.

"Where is he? Where is he? I'll kill him this time," she declared, waving the wooden spoon.

"No wonder the shopping cost so much this month!"

Fortune Favours the Brave

We'd play aeroplanes in the garden, and took turns as Da, holding a hand and a foot, spun us around real fast, with our heads rubbing the grass and the daisies. Da would laugh, and we'd be shouting till we got dizzy, and we loved doing that. But most of the time, we played football matches, and soon there was no grass left, only up along the sides. And sometimes there'd be fighting as well as football, and my glasses would have to go back to the man in town.

The Brother said that anyone who wanted to be in his gang had to be brave. I was kind of brave, but it didn't matter, because Ma said he had to play with me anyway. One day, he came home all excited from the posh school.

"I'm planning an adventure," he told the gang. "One lad in my class says there's a quarry up in Beaumont with caves in it. We'll go exploring on Saturday."

"Can I come, can I come?" Pudding Head, Tippy-Toes, and Plank asked.

"Yeah, but we'll have to make flaming torches to bring down the caves with us. They'll be like the ones we had when we were up in Uncle Eddie's. D'you remember them, Four Eyes?"

"Yeah, course I do."

The Brother gave everyone a nickname. Mine was Four Eyes, and I couldn't do anything about that. Ma told him to call me by my proper name. He never did. Johnny had a head like the bowl Ma used for baking, and that's why he was Pudding Head. Steve had a funny way of running, like a ballet dancer. That's why he was Tippy-Toes, and Frank was Plank because he was long like a telegraph pole and kind of thick as well.

All the gang were sitting around in a circle with their gobs open, listening to the Brother's plans.

"As we've no bulrushes, everyone must get something like a brush handle or a long stick and some rags, and we'll tie them to the end. We'll need to get petrol. Who can get petrol? And we need a rope?"

Silence. Nobody on our road had a car.

"I'll ask my Da if he can get us some at his work," said Liam, who wasn't yet a fully-fledged member of the gang and so was without a nickname.

"He's a mechanic and works in a garage."

"Ask him tonight. If he gets us some, you can come, but you'll still have to pass a bravery test to be in the gang."

Although Ma spent most of the time in the kitchen, she heard us planning the expedition and wasn't happy.

"Where's this quarry? Is it safe? What do you think, Da?"

"Yes, where is this so-called quarry?"

"It's up in Beaumont by my new friend's house, and everyone up there plays in it."

"Are you sure?"

"Yeah, swear to God."

"Well, if everyone plays there, I suppose it's OK."

"Can we have some rags, Ma, to make our torches?"

She went rummaging.

"Here, you can use these," she said, holding up a pair of knickers that were once pink. "The elastic is gone from all the washing. I was going to use them as dusters." And then she ripped them in two – one leg for me and one for the Brother. Ma had a big bum, so there was plenty.

"Thanks, Ma."

Liam delivered on the petrol and the rope. His Da was as excited as us and did a practice on the Friday before bedtime. He poured a tiny drop of petrol on a rag tied to a brush handle and lit it.

Whoosh.

Flames and black smoke took off like a rocket, nearly up to the moon. "Yahoo!" we shouted and ran around like Indians. Ma thought the whole thing was far too dangerous. She looked out the kitchen window and said the Rosary.

"We'll head off at zero nine hundred hours," our leader informed us, like a general in the army. "It'll be a long day, men, so bring sweets and stuff to eat."

Next morning, the Brother had us line up like soldiers on parade. He'd the rope slung over his shoulder, and a schoolbag filled with the bottle of petrol and other important things on his back.

"Right," he said, "nearly ready, except you've to do a bravery test, Liam."

"OK."

The Brother had Da's hatchet in his hand.

"Stand here, Liam, with your feet together like this. I'm after thinking up a new test. Now, I'm going to dig into the ground with a flake of the hatchet right next to you, and you're not to move an inch – OK?"

Liam nodded.

The hatchet buried itself in the earth. Liam jumped back.

"You can't be in the gang, you're not brave," the Brother told a shaking explorer.

"I am, I am, I swear I am. Gimme another chance."

And he gave him another go. And this time Liam didn't move, and this time the hatchet didn't bury itself in the ground. No, it buried itself in the toe of Liam's left shoe. And Liam fell... well, he didn't really fall, but he hopped around like a kangaroo and screamed his head off.

But Liam was kind of lucky. He was the only one not wearing sandals, and he was *really* lucky because his ma bought his new shoes "a bit on the big size", and when the bleeding stopped and he took off his blood-soaked sock,

126

only a bit of his nail had disappeared from his big toe. The Brother took out a long string of liquorice and gave it to Liam for being so brave. And his ma was nice and didn't give out to us for chopping off the top of his new shoe.

After the unscheduled delay, the expedition headed off at ten hundred hours, the Brother leading the way with an arm around Liam, who limped alongside, his face the colour of milk.

"You can be in my gang 'cos you were brave, and 'cos you only lost a teensy bit of your toe, I think we'll call you Lucky. Lucky Liam, OK?"

The Brother's friend from school met us and brought us to the quarry, past a "Danger! Keep Out!" sign, and another one, until, in behind another "Danger! No Entry!" sign, we saw a hole in the fence.

"Hurry and crawl through before someone sees us," our leader ordered.

"What about the signs?" I said, "I don't think Ma—"

"Well, go home so, Four Eyes."

I didn't know the way back, so I crawled through.

I thought we'd walk into a little cave, light our torches, have our picnic, and go home, and I didn't know why we needed a rope, but I was about to find out.

After climbing through long hairy grass and over millions of rocks as big as our house, the Brother's friend pointed to a hole about the same size as me, in between two humongous rocks.

"This is it," he said, pointing down. "Once you get through there, you must climb down, and at the bottom, the cave gets massive."

We stood at the edge, gawking into this black hole. Time for a wee.

"Right," said the Brother, leaving his schoolbag and torch on the ground. "Let's get going."

After he and his friend wrapped one end of the rope around the massive rock and tied loads of knots, he tied the other end around his belly and disappeared down the hole. Gone like a dog chasing a cat.

Seconds later we heard, "Throw down the torch and pull up the rope and tie my bag around it and lower it down and be careful with the petrol."

We followed the instructions of our leader.

"It's brilliant down here, the torch is working fab," an echoing voice from underground called up, giving us the latest news.

"Tie the rope around your bellies and climb down like I did. It's easy."

One by one, like commandoes, we descended. Me second last because I was only learning how to tie my shoelaces and wasn't too sure about tying knots in ropes, but I tied hundreds, moved to the edge, and headed down. It was like climbing a tree backwards. I took my time, feeling around with my toes for the next rock, and holding on tight, hoping I wouldn't fall and get clobbered, because I wasn't so sure about the knots.

I got there.

The Brother stood like a king, holding his flaming torch. The black smoke made me cough.

"Isn't this brill?" he said. "Don't light the rest till everyone's down."

I felt a shiver run down my back. The place scared me, and it smelled like bad eggs or cat's wee, and the roof leaked or else it was raining because I got soaked, and the corners were full of shadows jumping around from the flames, and they looked like ghosts. We could stand in the middle, but the Brother said we'd have to crawl on our bellies when we'd go exploring, and I wasn't sure I'd enjoy that.

One by one, the troops followed until it came to Liam, Lucky Liam.

"C'mon, you're the last one," the Brother shouted up. The echo bounced off the wet, slithery walls.

We didn't know it, but Liam wasn't a good knot-tier, because when halfway down, the rope came loose and he tumbled down, and hit his nut off two rocks.

He screamed and howled so loud I'd to put my fingers in my ears, and with the Brother's flickering torch we could see blood gushing from Liam's head through his fingers, and it dripped everywhere, and it looked like a Frankenstein picture.

"I'm going to die; I'll have no blood left."

"Nah," said Plank. "Anytime I get cut, my ma says we've got buckets of blood, yeah, buckets of the stuff, and it doesn't matter if you lose some."

I don't think Lucky Liam was convinced.

"Hang on," our leader ordered. "We'll get you fixed up. We'll use the rags from Four Eyes' torch to make a bandage." C'mere,' he said,."Don't stand there like an eejit, rip it off."

And we wrapped Ma's knickers around his forehead, and they turned a pinkish colour for the first time in years.

"We'll have to come back next week to do the exploring," the Brother said. "We can't go on with a wounded soldier." And one by one, we climbed up out of the cave. I was glad.

After we'd eaten our sweets, crisps and lemonade, the Brother, who had us sitting in a circle, said, "I've been thinking."

I didn't like when he started thinking because it usually ended up with trouble and Ma getting out the wooden spoon.

"I've been thinking that Lucky Liam needs a new name, and I think we'll call him Buckets o' Blood." And just like that, Liam became Buckets o' Blood.

And we marched back home along the Boreenmanna road, holding our torches up like spears, but they weren't lit or anything like that. Just pretend.

Then we'd more screaming when Liam's mother saw the state of him. The blood had dried on his face, hands, and head, and with Ma's knickers around his forehead, he looked like an Apache.

"Maybe it'd be safer to find someone else to play with," she told him later. "That crowd who've moved from Dublin seem wild or mad or maybe a bit of both."

Nah. Buckets o' Blood didn't desert us.

Never Count Your Chickens

Every Sunday, after Da had finished reading the *Sunday Independent*, but before he started cutting it up for bog paper, Ma took out the fashion page. Not that she was into the fashion or anything like that. Well… maybe she was, but that was only dreaming because she'd no spare money. But she always kept enough to do the Fashion Competition.

"'Tis my only little treat for the week."

Pictures of ladies in dresses or skirts or other stuff with a letter next to each one were spread across the page, A-B-C-D… all the way to L or M. Ma picked out the ones she thought were the nicest and filled out the box at the bottom. Three pence a line to enter. Ma usually did a shilling's worth.

"Could you imagine if I won? Janey Mackers, £500 or even a runners-up prize? The first thing I'd do would be to go into Roches Stores and buy a piece of carpet. I'd fed up with that lino and having a room carpeted would nearly make us posh. Then I'd get proper curta—"

"And would you buy us bikes, Ma?" the Brother asked.

"We'll have to win first. C'mon, let you have a go. You might have better luck. I'm doing it this past ten years, and not a brass farthing have I got from them blighters."

Every Monday, Ma headed to the post office up the road, bought a postal order and a stamp, and off went her entry, never to be heard of again.

Not until that Thursday, about a year after we'd landed in Cork.

It felt like the North Pole, and I'd run home, as I always did, to escape the enemy. My knees were red and sore from my hairy pants rubbing, and Ma wasn't in the kitchen where she should've been. No! She stood at the door going doolally, jumping up and down like there were springs in

131

her shoes and waving an envelope over her head like a loony.

"Look!" she said. "Look at this." And I looked. In each corner were big letters. I started – "S-u-n-d-"

"Never mind, never mind that. It's from the *Sunday Independent*."

"What does it say, Ma?"

"I don't know. We'll wait till Da and your brother come before opening it."

She'd forgotten about the bacon and cabbage in the saucepan until they started to stink, and she'd to open the kitchen door and window to let the smoke out, but she kept dancing about when Da and the Brother got off the bus.

She handed Da the envelope. He held it like it was a stick of dynamite and looked at the front and back of it a couple of times before opening it with his knife.

Dear Mrs O'Leary,

Thank you for the entry to last week's Fashion Competition. You completed two lines costing sixpence, but your postal order was for one shilling. Therefore, you overpaid, and we now have pleasure in enclosing a cheque for the balance.

I think the letter said some more things about wishing her good luck and all that auld shite, but Da didn't read it out loud.

Tears flowed down Ma's cheeks like it was pouring rain.

The smell of the cabbage got worse.

Wool and Water

"Can I go to the baths instead of having a bath, Ma?" the Brother started.

"What are you talking about?"

"The baths, the swimming baths in town. All the lads in my class go. Can I go next week, please, Ma? I swear I won't get into any trouble, and one of my friends said he'd lend me a pair of his togs."

"But you can't swim."

"I'll learn from the lads. Please, Ma, please."

"We'll ask your da when he comes home."

Once he'd been, the Brother never shut up about his first time in Eglinton Street baths.

"'Tis massive," he started. "A gigantic pool with a deep end, and down the other end, it's not deep and the young fellas splash around down there. And it's brilliant 'cos there're no girls. They've their own pool. We can't see them, but we can hear them giggling and screeching. And there's fat fellas in charge waddling around, making sure no one peeps around the corner to have a geek at them putting on their knickers."

Ma had given him sixpence. "You wouldn't want to be getting fond of the swimming at that price."

Later, he told me a secret. "Don't tell, Ma, or I'll kill you, but it's only a thruppenny bit to get in. I bought a cake with the other threepence. It's called Donkey's Gudge. They make them in the shop around the corner. Cuthbert's, it's called."

The Brother learned fierce quick, and after a few weeks, he told us he could swim all on his own from one side to the other.

"Well, that's great," Ma said. "Sure, can't you take your brother the next time and teach him?"

"Ah, Ma, he's not coming. He'd spoil everything, and anyway, he's no togs."

"Don't be getting cheeky. It doesn't suit you and don't worry about the togs. Hand me down that knitting basket."

Ma rummaged and found a ball of leftover wool and started.

Grey, they were. Hairy, itchy ones that made me scratch around my willie when she made me try them on.

"They'll do you grand. I've put in two bands of extra strong elastic to be sure."

They didn't look too bad, except for the tiny duck sewn into one leg.

Ma gave each of us an old towel, and with our togs wrapped up inside, we took off, running for the baths, gripping our sixpenny pieces tightly in our fists.

Saturday, no school, and we headed for the 2 o'clock session. You could only stay for an hour, no matter how dirty you were or how many miles you wanted to swim. Everybody was supposed to queue, but that didn't stop a load of big fellas, bigger than the Brother, from pushing their way to the front.

"Don't even look at them," the Brother whispered. "D'you see the gait of them? They're from the North side. Right hard chaws, they are."

We gave our money to the man at the turnstile, and he gave us back our change. He looked half asleep and could have done with going for a swim himself. Behind him, a sign covered the whole wall. It said *No Running – No Jumping – No Cursing – No Spitting.* Underneath, someone had written *Or Else!*

"Hide the threepenny bit in your sock," the Brother said. "Those gurriers steal everything and would do anything."

I wasn't even inside and I was beginning to think this might be even worse that dealing with Chimp at school.

The Brother hadn't told lies. The pool was bigger than our garden, and the smell made my eyes burn.

"They dump stuff called chlorine into the water to stop it going the colour of wee 'cos everyone does one, and if they didn't put in the smelly stuff, we'd all get a dose of the shits."

Benches went all the way around, and after taking off our duds and getting into our togs, we wrapped our clothes in our towels so they wouldn't get soaked. I hid my money and specs in one of my sandals.

The noise was worse than thunder as hundreds jumped in and started screeching and messing around.

Ready, but not willing, I stood at the side, chewing my lip, shivering, turning into a giant goose pimple.

The Brother swam about in the deep end and saw no reason I wouldn't join him.

"C'mon, you eejit, just jump in."

Splash!

I was in. *Pushed* in.

I sank.

Because I'd opened my gob, I swallowed hundreds of gallons of chlorine-laced water, but came back up, and grasped the railing. My heart tried to escape. Then someone grabbed and pulled me out.

"Are you thick or something? What the feck are you doing in the deep end?"

One of the fat lifeguards kept shouting and made me touch my toes millions of times till I got sick. I was going to tell him about the boy who pushed me, but I saw him looking at me like a gangster, and I knew by the way he looked, he'd have chopped off my head if I said anything.

Then I noticed. Ma's elastic had worked. The wool didn't. The bit with the extra strong elastic stayed around my belly, but I watched as the sodden mess sagged the duck down to my ankles.

135

"Ah, Janey Mackers," said the Brother. "You look like you've done a load, and you look a right eejit."

I cried and wished Ma had stuck to the Aran sweaters.

"Everyone out. Everyone get out now," roared not one but the two lifeguards.

"Look," said the Brother, "look over there, down at the bottom. Someone's done a shit in the pool."

Without my specs, I had to squint, but spotted it down in a corner a little bit from where I'd been swallowing water.

"Stand back," said one lifeguard as he peered into the pool.

"Get dressed and feck off, the lot of ye," said the other, but nobody stirred.

"Don't worry, mister. I'll get it out," came from across the now half-empty pool and before anyone could say or do anything, the fella who pushed me was swimming underwater towards the perfectly formed crap.

He grabbed it, surfaced, leapt out, and started eating it.

The two lifeguards vomited into the pool, so the emptying had to continue.

The Brother never stopped laughing all the way home.

"That was the funniest thing ever, wasn't it? Your man sitting at the edge eating the Punch bar, but he must be as thick as shit 'cos he's barred forever."

After we stopped to get our Donkey's Gudge, he told me he'd never again take me.

"You're like a Jonah."

That suited me. I'd decided that staying alive was more important than swimming with all the corner boys. I took a bite of cake and said nothing.

I told Ma what happened with the togs. She must've felt sorry for me and gave me another threepence.

"Get yourself an ice-cream or a little cake."

And I thought it best not to tell her about eating Donkey's Gudge. I got a cream and jam éclair and sat on our wall. A lick of cream first, then a bite, then a lick of jam, and it took me ages to eat it because I saw the Brother peeping out, and I knew he was dying to ask for a bite, but wouldn't.

The togs stayed in our house for years. Ma used them for dusting.

Romance

There were loads of girls on our road, and they got in the way. They'd be playing with prams and dolls and other stuff, and hadn't a clue, because a few times they even tried to play hopscotch where we needed to play football. Sometimes after it'd rained for days, our garden got all mucky, and all the grass down the middle was gone, and we'd skeet and slide on our arses all over the place. That's why we'd to play on the road. And the stupid girls didn't understand. One day, one of them, the chubby one, Mary Cream Cakes, even asked me and Frank the Plank to play house.

"Play house? You must think we're thick or something," Plank said, and it sounded funny to hear Frank saying something about being stupid.

I never told the lads, because they would have laughed, but sometimes, when Ma dragged me along to Mrs Walsh's for a cuppa, I played with Goldie Locks. Alice was her proper name, and she wasn't the girl who'd showed me her knickers. She wore pink glasses. We played mas and das and dressed up in old clothes and even played pillow fights. But I never played with dolls.

Our road had a high wall at the end. Da called it a posh name – "It's a cul-de-sac. That's French," he told us. My Da knew lots of things because he wore a suit all the time.

In behind the wall was a fantastic place for playing war games, and cowboys, and hide 'n' seek. First, you'd get a bunk up, then hang over the side by your fingers, close your eyes, and drop into the long grass. Nettles and thorny things grew there, but we cleared paths and made camps and everything.

Steve's ma gave us a gigantic piece of lino after she got posh and bought a carpet for their good room. We cut it and used some to make a roof in between the branches, and we sat on the other bit and had meetings.

We got braver, going further and further, looking for adventure and mischief.

"I heard from a fella who heard it from another fella who knows someone who nearly had his leg bitten off by wild dogs that live way up in the woods," Johnny Pudding Head told us. "Maybe we should plan for a quick escape... just in case."

We nodded like wise old men.

"I'll be back in a minute," said Frank. Five minutes later, he returned with thick pieces of wood – a short bit, a middling-sized bit, and a long plank.

"We'll put these up against the wall and can use them as steps to get out."

Maybe 'tis time Frank got a new nickname, I thought.

The Brother didn't play with us so much anymore. He'd started putting Brylcream in his hair and aftershave on his face. I thought that was stupid because he didn't even shave.

Ma nearly wore out her finger from wagging it at him.

"Where are you going?"

"Out."

"Out where?"

"Nowhere."

"And what're you doing out there?"

"Nothing."

"Gimme patience. I don't know why your father is wasting his money on that school. The only words I'm getting out of you are 'out' an' 'nothing'."

Me and my gang headed further into the woods, single file, like commandoes, listening and watching out for the mad dogs. Frank spotted them first. Not the dogs, but apple trees. Apple trees with millions of apples, and a house.

139

"Shhh," I told my comrades. "Get down on your bellies and wait till we see if anyone's around."

We waited till Pudding Head jumped up.

"There's some fecking thing after crawling up the leg of me khakis."

Our cover blown, we stood and watched him do a war dance, one hand up the leg of his trousers, rummaging.

"It'll be up by my willie if I don't find it!"

He found it. A tiny spider.

"You fecking dope," I said. "You could've got the lot of us captured."

The house looked sad with a tree growing in the chimney, and weeds as big as me flapped at the windows. All the curtains were closed, and there were no dogs. I thought of Mango and wondered if he missed me, because I missed him.

We started. First, we tucked our jumpers inside our pants and started picking. And we didn't even have to climb up to get them. I stuffed two big ones inside my jumper.

"You look like you've got titties," said Frank.

After a few minutes, with our pullovers sticking out, we looked like we'd babies in our bellies.

"We'll come back tomorrow for more and don't be telling anyone else," I ordered the troops.

We emptied our stash on the footpath; green ones, reddish ones, and some that birds had tried. All of them were lousy.

"We risked our lives for cookers, fecking cookers," said Frank, as if we didn't know.

My Da was fiercely honest. Once he found a pencil from his work in my pencil case.

"This is the property of the company, Son. I could be in serious trouble if someone saw you using company property in school."

140

Because Da was honest, Ma had to be as well, but she didn't lecture me when I presented her with the apples.

"We'll keep it a secret," she said, and we'd apple tart every day for weeks.

Frank had a secret as well.

"Your man in the shop sells fags."

"That's not news, you clown. We know he sells cigarettes," I said, putting him straight.

"But you didn't know he sells them in 1s, did you?"

Now he had our attention.

Frank gave out the details.

"My brother, who's ten and a half, gets them nearly every day. Friar Tuck keeps a box under the counter and will sell you one, two, or three."

We collected pennies and Frank, who, like the rest of us, was eight and a bit, but taller, volunteered to carry out the mission.

"Try to be all relaxed, like," I told him. "Whistle when you go in and buy the gobstoppers first. Then ask for the fag."

I sent Johnny Pudding Head home to steal a box of matches. Ma never left matches lying around our house after my previous adventure.

Frank presented us with a single Capstan Navy Cut Full Strength. In over the wall with the lot of us. By now, we were experts at going in and out of the woods. We'd made steps on both sides.

As the leader of our gang, I got first drag, and when my head started spinning, I sat down, but pretended nothing. All the lads had a go, but none seemed eager to have a few more pulls.

When I got home Ma said, "You're looking very pasty. What's up with you?"

"Nothing." I'd learned a lot from the Brother.

I pretended I needed a wee and put toothpaste in my mouth in case Ma came close and smelt me.

Someone must have been boasting though, because the stupid girls heard what we'd done, and Creamy Cakes said she'd tell if we didn't give them a try.

I knew we should've just hit them, but we'd have probably got a walloping for that, so we brought them along.

They hadn't a clue how to smoke. And it got worse. They started climbing over our wall on their own and playing in the camps we'd made.

"I've a new game. Would you like to play?" Alice asked when we were all sitting around.

"It's called Dare, Truth, Kiss, Command or Promise."

I said nothing but looked over at Liam. His face turned the colour of a tomato, and Frank started picking at the scab on his knee, while Steve and Johnny looked at the ground.

"Let's try it once," said Alice. "I'll close my eyes and do a twirl and when I stop, I'll point at someone, and he'll have to kiss me."

Round and round she went. I'm sure she got dizzy, and after wobbling a bit, she straightened herself and her glasses and pointed. At me.

All the lads started jeering and clapping and I hadn't a clue what to do, but Alice, Goldie Locks, did. I stood up, and she came and tried to kiss me, but our glasses started fencing and fell off.

"This is a stupid game," I told the gang. "Come on, let's get our rifles and bows and arrows and head off."

It took weeks, but Alice kept us practicing till we got it right. But once when I touched her lips, they were all sticky because she'd just finished eating a sherbet dip, and I preferred playing cowboys.

Lift an' Shift!

"It's like a giant Easter egg," said Frank.

"Nah," said Pudding Head, "'tis more like a flying saucer."

I think Ma got it right when she said Miss McNamara's car looked like a giant wasp when she drove down the road in her span-new yellow Bubble car with a black roof. Nearly as exciting as the day the circus came to the parish field. All the neighbours came out to have a gawk at the first car on our road.

"No fear of anyone getting rolled over by that yoke," said Da. "I've seen a hedgehog with sore toes move faster. An' anyway, it's not a proper car really, with only three wheels. I'd say it's as light as a feather."

"Really, Da?"

"Yeah, I'd say it wouldn't take much to lift it."

Not only did Miss McNamara own the only car on our road, but she was the only one with a proper garden with flower beds, and when she wasn't polishing the Bubble, she'd spend nearly every Saturday on her hands and knees hunting for daisies. And she never smiled or said hello to anyone, and Ma said she'd seen more personality on a blank page.

And she robbed footballs.

Our footballs.

"Frustrated. That's what's wrong with that one," Ma said. "She's full of herself. I don't know where she gets the notions. 'I'm working for *Bank of Ireland*' and all that auld shite. Did you ever see her? Waddling her backside, an' her front as flat as the ironing board. Probably no fella good enough for her. What that one needs is a farmer. A Kerry farmer with the muscles of a bullock who'd keep her warm in bed an' put a smile on that puss of hers."

"What does 'frustrated' mean, Ma?"

"Eat your dinner. You'll learn soon enough."

"Maybe she should get a hot water bottle," said the Brother.

"Don't you be getting smart, or you'll get a clip around the ear."

"Jerry thinks she could be a bit of a dark horse," Da said, with a grin spreading across his face.

"Does he now? And is that all ye have to talk about? A pair of dirty old men, that's what ye are," Ma replied, folding her arms, which wiped the grin off Da's puss.

The Brother was on a bit of a run and leapt in with; "You're not dirty, Da. Sure, don't you have a bath every Saturday?"

This time, his newfound wit earned him a wallop around the back of his head.

"It's a pity you're not so clever at school."

Every Friday, and most other nights, Da went to The Orchard for a few pints with Jerry. He owned the shop and allowed Ma to buy on tick, and like the taxi driver who used to take us to Uncle Eddie's, he'd a short leg, but I don't think they were cousins or even knew each other.

Ma said she could never figure out how Da and Jerry became such good friends.

"Sure, all the pair of you do is plonk themselves down, sip pints, smoke fags, and not a dozen words pass between the pair of you."

Knitting and keeping an eye on things was Ma's way of relaxing. Like a sentry, she'd sit inside the living room window, needles clattering and fencing like Zorro, all the time keeping a watch through the net curtains on who was going or coming.

The Brother didn't play with us much since he'd made a new friend. The mirror. Hours he'd spend in the jacks, combing his hair or searching his face for pimples.

"If you keep at that nose of yours," Ma said, "you'll end up like Bozo the Clown. 'Tis big enough as it is."

And Da issued instructions. "Don't be locking that door unless you're doing Number Two."

With our road being a cul-de-sac, no lorries or buses bothered us, and we'd play matches from one end to the other. Hundreds of us. We used jumpers as goals and anytime some eejit kicked a gammy shot into a garden, he'd leap over the wall or gate to get it. Unless it was Miss McNamara's garden, and she was at home. She kept her gate locked, and we never figured out how, but as soon as the ball landed, she'd spring from nowhere and grab it.

"Don't you know that playing football on the road is against the law and you nearly broke my lovey narcissi? Now clear off or I'll call the guards."

Sometimes she gave us back the ball, but that stopped the day Johnny stuck out his tongue and said the effer word.

And on my birthday, Ma and Da bought me a new football. A full size, no 5, like big footballers use. A week later, Frank, the eejit, kicked it into Miss McNamara's and it hopped off the roof of her car. He opened the gate. It didn't squeak like all the others, and like a robber, he tiptoed up the driveway and was about to pick up my shiny new ball when she pounced.

"Get out." Her voice was sharp and strong like mustard, and I watched as she stabbed my ball with a carving knife.

I carried home the corpse and presented it to Ma, who got all het up.

Whipping off her *You'll Eat It and You'll Enjoy It* apron, she headed for the door.

"I'll sort out that cow."

Although the sun had stretched out its arms and had us all roasting, Ma picked up an umbrella. Not the small pink one, but Da's black one with the blackthorn handle. Da said it was double-ribbed, whatever that meant.

"Hold tough a minute," he said when he appeared from behind *The Independent.* "Technically, the bitch is right. The lads shouldn't be playing ball on the road."

"Whose side are you on?" said Ma, jabbing the umbrella like a sword. "I've always said there are three things needed for a happy life; a decent bit of food on the table, a good fire in the grate, and friendly neighbours, and I'm not letting that one spoil my hat-trick."

"Take it easy, Dear. Fighting on the street like Travellers isn't the answer."

"And what'll we do?"

"Nothing. We'll do nothing. Apples will grow again."

"What apples, Da?"

"It's a figure of speech, Son. Now, Mother, dish out the stew. We'll get another ball at the end of the month and from now on, play in the garden."

Da wasn't one for long speeches, but he was the boss and that was the end of that.

It was a Saturday morning in August, just before we went back to school, and Da didn't get up for his breakfast. I heard Ma saying something about giving him an ear-full because he didn't come home till all hours. Me and the Brother were eating our porridge when she nearly stuck her head through the window.

"Where's he off to at this hour, I wonder?"

"Who, Ma?"

"That's Guard Flynn gone down the road on his bike. There must be trouble."

We'd gobbled down the porridge and were out the door before she'd finished.

"Don't be so nosey, the pair of you," she said, but was on our heels, and the curlers still in her hair.

We spotted the high nelly bike resting against Miss McNamara's gate. Guard Flynn, a sound man according to Da, stood on the steps to the front door, writing at a fierce rate in a notebook the size of a cigarette box. Miss McNamara had gone crazy.

She jumped up and down and her arms flapped about like a chicken trying to take off. Flynn pushed back his hat and scratched his forehead. He looked at Miss McNamara's car.

It wasn't where it should be.

No. The car sat plonked on the flower bed in the middle of the garden, right where the daffodils used to be.

It seemed to be happy there.

Soon all my gang and the other mams and dads came along for a decko, and someone even took a photo.

They made inquiries at a few doors, but nobody knew anything. Guard Flynn got my da and three of the neighbours, after they'd stopped laughing, to lift the car back into the driveway.

Ma thought it the best thing in years.

"Seeing the look on her face was better than going to see *The Three Stooges*," she declared. As a treat she made us drop scones and drowned them with Golden Syrup and we'd roasting hot cups of tea as well.

"I wonder who moved it?" said Ma. "Somebody must know."

"Obviously, Dear."

"I wonder who it was?"

Da said nothing, but while Ma cleared up the plates, he looked over, winked, and said, "Looks like the apples have grown again, Son."

I tried to wink but wasn't good at that. But in both Da's confidence, and in my understanding of it, I knew I'd soon be a big boy.

Getting the Flu

One day, during the summer holidays, Frank told me we were doing the kissing all wrong. He'd loads of bigger sisters and took peeks at their comics, ones like *Jackie* and *Tammy*.

"You have to lie on top to do it right."

"What?"

"Yeah, you get them to lie on the grass and climb on top and kiss them."

Frank ran the idea past Mary Cream Cakes, promising her two strings of liquorice. I think he'd have got away with one, but she'd only go if Alice went and that's how I got dragged along.

"Why can't you lie on the grass?" she asked.

"Cos Frank says the boy must be on top."

"But there might be nettles and creepy crawlies."

So, I took off my jumper and laid in on the grass. She walked around it three times like a dog before she lay down and closed her eyes.

I did as Frank told me, but all I could see was up her nose and there was a snot hanging at the corner, so I got up and ran away. And I left my pullover after me.

Weeks later, as it got dark, me and Frank sat under the streetlamp outside his house. Ma allowed me to stay out because we hadn't gone back to school yet. And Frank had a bundle of comics. Some cowboy and war ones, but he'd sneaked out one called *True Romance*. It was cold sitting on the footpath in khaki shorts, but I didn't mind. We looked at the pictures with loads of kissing and stuff and then something happened, and I ran home again.

"Ma, Ma! My willie went all stiff."

Da disappeared behind the *Evening Press*.

"Don't worry, love," Ma said. "You must've got a chill. Maybe 'tis the flu. Put on your jammies and I'll make a cup of cocoa to warm you up."

The cocoa worked, but I got the flu a lot after that.

One night at the start of December, Ma stayed in the kitchen after we'd had beans on toast for tea. She'd to get the almond paste and icing ready for the Christmas cake. Da and me huddled by the fire, me reading a comic, and Da chewing the end off a pencil trying to finish the crossword. The Brother foostered around with the radio. Our contraption, the size of a suitcase, sat on a table in the corner by the window, took ages to warm up and worked when it felt like it.

"Jeez, what's that racket?" Da asked, dropping the paper and covering his ears.

"I've got it, Da. I've got radio Luxembourg."

"Turn it down, will you? What's all that screeching?"

"Da, that's Elvis! You know, Elvis Presley."

"I don't care who or what he is, turn him down or preferably off."

"But Da, Elvis is famous, and he'll soon be Number 1 in the world."

"Now Son, you take it from me here and now, that fella's roaring and shouting will never catch on. Your man Elvis or whatever his name is will never make it. He'll be forgotten about this time next year."

Da took a long pull on his cigarette and flicked the ash in the general direction of the fireplace.

I'd moved on from *The Beano* and was reading a war story in *The Victor* when Da leant over and asked, "Will you be writing to Santa this year?"

I said nothing but gave him the look.

"Thought so. Me and your Mother are thinking it's about time we got you a pair of long trousers. We'll get them when I get paid before Christmas."

And then I really was a Big Boy.

~~~~~~~~~

About the Author

After taking early retirement, Eamon realised he needed something more than hacking up the golf course to keep himself occupied and started writing. Better with pen than the club, his award-winning stories have been widely published, capturing the imagination of editors on both sides of the Atlantic.

With a nicely jaundiced, but fond eye on the past Eamon combines humour and sentiment in equal measure, exquisitely mining the diamond moments of a child growing up in 1960s Ireland.

His humorous vignettes make him a regular (broadcaster) on the national airways, as a contributor to *A Word in Edgeways* on RTE Radio1.

The proud father of Susan and Lynn and grandad to Theo, Lennon, Archie, and Harley. Nothing gives him greater pleasure than helping the grandkids get into mischief they haven't even thought of yet!

Acknowledgements

The author alone doesn't bring a book to life. It's a team effort, with many people contributing in a myriad of sometimes small but important ways.

I've had this collection of childhood memories rattling around in my cranium for yonks, and it was only after I retired and quickly realised I needed something more than hacking up the golf course to fill my days that I put pen to paper.

Like a child heading off to school on his first day, I nervously took my first effort to a meeting of Carrigaline Writers. They liked it. Special thanks to Patsy Goulding and Bernie Healy for their encouragement.

Weeks later, it felt as if I'd won the Lottery when John Dolan published the story in *The Holly Bough*. Thanks, John.

I met Tony Fyler via the now defunct YouWriteOn writing group. What a discovery. He is a truly wonderful editor who, as well as prompting, poking and correcting my efforts, kept me going when on occasions, my confidence dipped.

A special mention to the library service in Cork County Council for setting up the wonderful Writer in Residence programme. Danny Denton was inspirational.

My most sincere thanks to the gifted award-winning writer, Billy O'Callaghan, who took me under his wing and greatly helped in getting the book over the finish line.

Thanks to Matt at Pure Slush Books, who previously published two of the stories, *Bells a Ringing* and *The Stiff-Legged Walk*.

And of course, thanks to Gill James and the Bridge House Publishing team for taking me on my first journey through the publishing minefield and producing my legacy.

Like to Read More Work Like This?

Then sign up to our mailing list and download our free collection of short stories, *Magnetism*. Sign up now to receive this free e-book and also to find out about all of our new publications and offers.

Sign up here:
    http://eepurl.com/gbpdVz

Please Leave a Review

Reviews are so important to writers. Please take the time to review this book. A couple of lines is fine.

Reviews help the book to become more visible to buyers. Retailers will promote books with multiple reviews.

This in turn helps us to sell more books... And then we can afford to publish more books like this one.

Leaving a review is very easy.

Go to https://amzn.to/4dPCGPq, scroll down the left-hand side of the Amazon page and click on the 'Write a customer review' button.

Other Publications by Bridge House

Old Man Jasperson
by Jim Bates

In this collection, Jim looks into what it means to be human in this day and age. How do we cope with the loss of a loved one? What brings us joy? How important is friendship? Can Nature heal?

These are heavy questions, and Jim tackles them head-on with stories that are both intriguing and entertaining. He is not afraid to delve deep into life's challenges. He looks at love and loss, our hopes and dreams, and our own inner fears. Ultimately, his stories show us the strength of the human character.

These stories are heartfelt, and told with quiet passion and a gentle touch. In the end, they resonate with Jim's appreciation for the challenges we all face and, ultimately, the beauty of what it means to be truly alive and to live in this world.

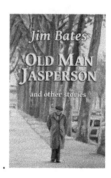

Order from Amazon:

Paperback: ISBN 978-1-914199-46-2
eBook: ISBN 978-1-914199-47-9

The Story Weaver
by Sally Zigmond

Story-telling has often been associated with weaving and
spinning. All is craft, cleverness and magic.

Here indeed we have a colourful mix of beautifully crafted
stories. Some are sad and others bring us hope. There are
tensions in relationships, fear of the unknown coupled with
surprising empathy, and accidents of birth. Death wishes are
reversed, sometimes but not always, and so are lives in other
realties. People's stories intersect as they wait for a bus. An old
cello causes havoc. A church clock always strikes twice… or
does it? Match-making goes wrong until it goes right. And so
much more.

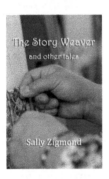

"A wonderful collection of interesting tales. A real mixture
that will delight all readers." *(Amazon)*

Order from Amazon:

Paperback: ISBN 978-1-914199-54-7
eBook: ISBN 978-1-914199-55-4

The Adventures of Iris and Zach
by I.L. Green

Iris and Zach have an uneasy but intriguing run.

A vast patchwork landscape of life is displayed through stories relating both the wonder and absurdity we all recognize. With a focus on mental health, these stories take the reader from incarceration to freedom, fear to comfort. There are celebrations of life and poetic lows. The Yin and Yang aspects of life are recognized in new and deliberate examples that instil thoughtfulness and occasionally a smile.

Order from Amazon:

Paperback: ISBN 978-1-914199-34-9
eBook: ISBN 978-1-914199-35-6